No Peace of Mind

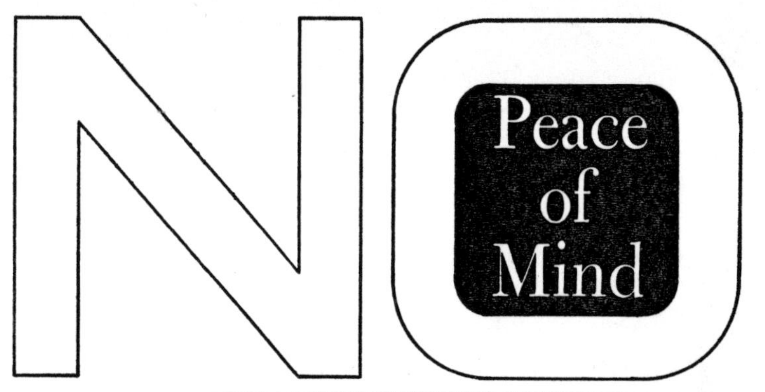

by Harry C. Meserve

Harcourt, Brace and Company HB New York

first edition

Library of Congress Catalog Card Number: 58-10902

Printed in the United States of America

To the men, women, and children of the First Unitarian Society of San Francisco in grateful remembrance and abiding affection

Contents

No Peace of Mind

Introduction The Anxious Man

A man walks in and sits down in the minister's study. He is well dressed, well mannered, and quiet in his speech.

"I do not know what is the matter with me," he says. "I really have nothing to worry about, but I worry all the time just the same. I have a good job, but I'm not sure how long it will last because our latest efficiency survey suggested some sweeping changes. I have a happy home life, too, but I may have to pull up stakes soon if I want to win a promotion. We really do have enough money to live on now, but everything seems to cost more and more all the time. I suppose I have most everything a man needs to be secure in this world, but who knows what this will be like soon if the politicians keep on messing things up? I cannot sleep. I seem constantly to worry about little things that should not matter at all. But sometimes I suspect they may point to something real, something dreadful. I no longer take much pleasure in my work or in my home. Somehow they don't mean much any more. Worst of all, I can't seem to put my finger on the real cause of most of these worries of mine. Maybe even if I could, I couldn't do much about it. I have even contemplated suicide in recent weeks, and I keep wondering whether life means anything at all in the long run. What is the matter with me? What can I do?"

We talk a long time and establish two facts: first, that this man's worries and fears *are not* abnormal, but thoroughly normal and, indeed, an integral part of the nervous and physical equipment inherited from his animal forebears; and second, that these anxieties are especially characteristic of the times in which we now live. This man, like the rest of us, is beset by disturbing circumstances which seem nearly impossible to change or overcome, even impossible to grasp in their entirety, and so doubly terrifying. Sensing the throng of inherent dangers but unable to visualize them accurately or to fight them on his own accustomed ground, bereft of belief in the simple faith which once sustained his fathers, he is, very understandably, in a state of primitive alarm. Since the dawn of history, men and animals have stood still in the face of unknown dangers, muscles tensed, skin tingling, heart pounding. My caller is simply a normal man of the mid-twentieth century, a typical victim of the anxious age, faced with its harrowing dilemma, a multitude of dangers not clearly perceived, never before encountered, and enormous in scope. He is lost in a bewildering forest and nowhere can be heard the song of the fabulous bird called Peace of Mind.

What should he do? Try larger and larger doses of pills to make him sleep and stimulants to wake him up? Reach ever more often for his private supply of tranquilizers? Indulge in longer and longer cocktail hours? Stickier and stickier doses of self-hypnotism beginning, "It's not so bad as you think," and continuing with, "There's really nothing to worry about"? Withdraw to the confines of his own gradually darkening mind, to escape a world he cannot face?

Or should he, rather, try to learn the real nature of his nameless fears, their origin and cause? Would it be fair to ask him, then, to face them manfully and correct them at the source? And, if the circumstances he fears are an unalterable part of the world of today, can he learn to accept without bitterness the uncertainties and dangers which have always been our human lot? Is there any hope that this spiritually displaced person may tap somewhere, somehow, new sources of inner strength?

The period since the end of the Second World War is now widely recognized, and even defined, as the Age of Anxiety. It has been a time when men and women have been beset, as never before in history, by a host of fears and persistent doubts, uncertainty as to the future of the world, and worry of all sorts as to their individual destinies. To list but a few of the specific anxieties which beset American men and women and young people today is to glimpse a world chaos seemingly endless in dimensions.

On the international front, there is the profound struggle between dictatorship and democracy. There is, also, an uneasy "peace" on a dozen different "fronts" which is no peace at all, but simply an absence of actual bloodshed. There is a host of new weapons with which, if war comes, man could destroy himself completely. Atomic weapons, hydrogen bombs, intercontinental missiles, sputniks, nuclear powered submarines, nerve gas, germ warfare—the list is long and ever longer. And moreover, even if our modern man manages to avoid physical destruction, he is increasingly aware that his mind may be the real target, and that it may eventually be overthrown by techniques of propaganda and "brainwashing" unknown in wars of previous centuries.

On the national front, the complexity of our modern society has forced us to be more dependent upon each other for the necessities of life than ever before in history. A strike in any basic industry can cripple the entire nation. An economic maladjustment in any one area can affect the total economy. The decisions of the Federal Reserve Board in Washington one month can control the contents of John Doe's paycheck on Main Street the following quarter. Factory workers, and executives too, can lose highly skilled and well paid jobs overnight in the constant process of streamlining which is part of our industrial progress. There are crushing tax burdens, a constantly spiralling inflationary process. It is easy to see the causes of anxiety which modern man faces in this area.

Add to these immediate financial worries the current insecurity which men and women face about the problems of old age, and we begin to glimpse the stark outlines of our neighbor's personal problem. What will become of him when he retires at the increasingly early age demanded by industry? Will his savings and pension be adequate to meet the costs of a constantly rising inflation? Will there be a place for him with his children, in the smaller homes which are characteristic of the modern generation? Indeed, will there be any place at all for him in the swiftly moving world at large, as his powers diminish? What will happen to his wife as she faces the long period of widowhood which seems to be the average fate of the American woman of the twentieth century?

To all these anxieties must be added the final, comprehensive one, which is most vague and yet most profoundly disturbing. We not only worry about how we shall survive, and how we personally fit into the general scheme of things; we wonder sometimes whether there is any scheme of things to fit into. Everyone sooner or later asks himself: "Do I matter at all? Do I have any worth, any real power and purpose as a person?" There is still another, more desperate question once posed by Macbeth. Is it possible that life is, after all, "a tale told by an idiot, full of sound and fury, signifying nothing"?

Professor Paul Tillich calls this the "anxiety of meaninglessness." It is the haunting feeling that in spite of all the demands of life, its desperate struggles, its moments of joy and fulfillment, its ever recurring sorrows and losses, the whole process may not point anywhere at all. And thus we see that the Age of Anxiety is basically one in which, in spite of all our powers and possibilities, we are unsure of the foundations of meaning beneath our lives. We know that we are in a period of transition. We know that the old verities do not seem to suffice, but we have as yet no new verities with which to replace the old ones.

It is this hunger for meaning, more than any other single force, which has brought the largest number of Americans in history into some sort of relationship with religious organizations and churches, and called forth the rebirth of interest in religion in our time. Vaguely aware that something is wrong—perhaps in themselves, perhaps in the world, perhaps in both—men have most understandably turned to religion to see if it can tell them what and where that "something" is. Most understandably, also, they yearn not only for a clarification of their dangers but for a method whereby they may be met and mastered.

In this book, we shall consider some of the facts about the so-called religious revival, and some of the antidotes to anxiety which are currently being offered in the name of religion. It will be important to keep certain questions in mind. What is the real function of religion? Is it the soothing of the troubled mind, or the arousing of the troubled mind to creative action and faith? Is anxiety a wholly evil and negative thing, or does it perhaps have some creative possibilities of its own? Do we really wish to remove anxiety and fear from our experience entirely, even if it were possible for us to do so? Or should these age-old emotions be used to stimulate the growth and enlarge the horizons of the human spirit?

Finally, what is the real task of religion in our modern world: to create an atmosphere of religious "authority" which flourished in bygone generations, to foster a return to the "fundamentalism" of our forefathers? Or should religion seek to guard us from dangers and give us peace of mind by the bland process of maintaining that danger does not exist? Or, simply and humbly and realistically, should religion seek to endow the individual with sharpened perception, that he may see the dangers of the modern world, and see them whole? And, most importantly, is it not the central task of religion today to endow man with renewed faith in himself and his universe, so that he might have the courage to make the mighty effort towards survival?

One ■ The New Piety

"If your church is not full today," a colleague in the ministry said to me not long ago, "it is because you are driving them away." He was essentially right. There is a renewed interest in religion in America today. Many, perhaps even most people, feel that they "ought to belong to a church"—if not for themselves then for the sake of their children. Those who are unable or unwilling to acknowledge their own personal need will frankly admit that they do not want their children to be without a religious point of view. And so, while bewildered themselves, they will faithfully bring their children to a church school and insist that they at least be taught the religious values which the parents dare not acknowledge that they too need. It is a further projection of the traditional American hope: "I want my child to have something better than I had."

The outward signs of a reawakening of interest in religion are numerous and familiar. The National Council of Churches' *Yearbook of American Churches* lists impressive statistics about the growth in church affiliation. Today, for the first time in history, there are more than 100 million Americans who are affiliated with churches or synagogues. Church membership has increased by 2.8 per cent as compared with a 1.8 per cent increase in population. A century ago less than 20 per cent of the population was church-affiliated. In 1900, the figure was 36 per cent. In 1940 it was 49 per cent, and in 1950, 57 per cent. Today it is 62 per cent. Protestantism—still the dominant religion of America—in 258 sects numbers approximately 58,500,000 adherents. The Roman Catholics claim about 33,400,000 souls, and Eastern Orthodox and dissenting Catholic groups just under 3,000,000. There are 5,500,000 Jews.

Church attendance is definitely up. Though accurate figures are not available, most clergymen will tell you that they have noticed a definite increase in their congregations during recent years. Per capita contributions to churches have risen markedly—7 per cent over the past year. There is a building boom in religious circles, and millions of dollars have been spent in the erection of new sanctuaries, education buildings, and parish houses. Ministers' salaries have increased to the point where a man starting out as a minister can expect to do as well or better than a man starting out as a teacher.

On college campuses chapels are well attended and courses in religion are booming. The Reverend Billy Graham, whose courage and sincerity nobody can deny, has made an impressive record in carrying his gospel to thousands of persons across the land and has won thousands to an acceptance of his fundamentalist interpretation of Christianity. But even Graham has a new rival so far as box office appeal goes. The Reverend Oral Roberts, a faith healer from Oklahoma, is now heard on 600 radio stations weekly and seen on 167 television stations. A small house for Roberts is 12,000, and par is between 15,000 and 16,000. A recent estimate of his television, radio, and short-wave audiences embraced almost one billion people. Unlike the deliberately modest salary of Mr. Graham, Roberts' annual income is reported to be about $100,000. Plainly, religion is becoming good box office and big business, at least for its more spectacular practitioners.

Figures of growth over the past five years reveal some interesting facts. The major, middle-of-the-road Protestant denominations have maintained a rate of growth about the same as that of the general over-all rate,—2.8 per cent. In some cases it is higher, in some lower. The Assemblies of God have nearly doubled their membership in five years. The Pentecostal Holiness Church shows a 50 per cent increase; the United Pentecostal Church something over 500 per cent, and the Pentecostal Assemblies of the World nearly 1200 per cent. The Roman Catholics have increased by over 20 per cent. Interestingly, at the liberal end of the religious spectrum, Unitarian growth over the past five years has been about 25 per cent.

Church membership figures are tricky. They are notoriously inaccurate since most local churches carry numerous deadwood names on their lists. The standards of membership vary widely. Some churches, like the Roman Catholic, count all baptized persons and admit of no withdrawals or resignations. Most Protestant churches count only those persons who have by their own will affiliated with the church, thus excluding children under the age of thirteen or fourteen. Yet perhaps we may venture one generalization. The most rapid growth seems to be taking place in the churches and religious fellowships which are essentially fundamentalist and authoritarian in their approach to religion. In a 1954 study conducted by the American Institute of Public Opinion, Princeton, New Jersey, a sample of adults was asked this question: Figures show that there are more people going to church these days. How do you account for this increase in church going? The replies were as follows:

Fear, unrest, uncertainty of future	30%
Renewed faith in God	19%
Postwar reaction	11%
Improved church programming and publicity	9%
Eisenhower influence	2%
Miscellaneous	1[illegible]%
Don't know	22%

Fear, unrest, and uncertainty of the future seem to be the major factors which are bringing about the renewed interest in religion; and, quite characteristically, that interest is directed towards the more dogmatic and authoritarian religious bodies.

Not long ago I was talking with a distinguished professor of history and philosophy in a nearby college. I asked him what signs he saw of a religious awakening on the campus. He replied that there undoubtedly was a greater interest in religion than he had ever seen before and that it showed itself mainly in a hunger for certainty. When people are fearful, anxious, uncertain, their first impulse is to seek some final and authoritative answers. Graham can give you Jesus, and Jesus can make you whole. Roberts can make you healthy. Peale can make you successful. The Bible contains the final answers. Obedience to the church can make you safe, both now and in eternity. What alluring answers for tired minds and anxious souls!

But there is a real question about the kind of religion being revived in the new piety. Is it a discovery of a deep ethical faith and of the resources of courage and strength which can enable us to meet the severe challenges of this time? Or is it a more or less superficial interest in certain outward signs and gestures without the deep inward changes of mind and spirit which always mark a revival of genuine religion?

The new piety takes various forms. One of them is the peace-of-mind, peace-of-soul variety. For millions of people who have left behind the "faith of our fathers" and have found little or nothing to put in its place, there is a great need for reassurance and for self-confidence.

There can be no doubt whatsoever that their anxiety is real and justified and that their need and hunger are sincere. But what does the new piety of peace of mind and soul offer them? It says in effect: "Everything is really all right. It is you who are out of tune with the Infinite. If you can just get right with God, cooperate with Him, get Him on your side, so to speak, then the things you want and have striven for so far with such disappointment can be yours. Your anxieties will be relieved. Your frustrations will be removed, and you will be on the way to success and happiness."

In this form of the new piety, religion appears as a means to an end. It justifies itself because it is useful to us in getting the things that we want and adjusting ourselves to the world. It helps us to "stop worrying and start living" or to get that promotion or to smooth out that unpleasant situation in our personal relationships.

All these things are undoubtedly good and necessary. But religion which is primarily a means of getting the things that we want belongs in the realm of magic. It is a primitive religion. The more mature and highly developed religions have insisted for centuries that the best and truest experiences of religion come when a person has given up asking "What do I require of God?" and learned to ask humbly "What does God require of me?"

Peace of mind, self-confidence, courage, strength, and faith are all precious spiritual gifts. All of us want and need more of them than we have. But if there is one consistent lesson of our historic religious tradition, both in Judaism and in Christianity, it is that these gifts come as by-products of our sincere and humble commitment to the task of doing justly, loving mercy, and walking humbly with our God.

It is a strange and persistent paradox of man's religious experience that his peace of mind and his courage and strength lie on the other side of his faithful commitment to purposes and ends larger and more durable than his personal destiny, and so worthy of his loyalty that he is able to give himself to them come what may. Jesus stated this paradox in two arresting passages: "Come unto me all ye that labor and are heavy-laden, and I will give you rest. Take my yoke upon you, and learn of me." That is to say, take up something of my labors; and in them, mysteriously, you will find the rest which you could not find elsewhere. Again, in even more familiar words: "Whoever will save his life shall lose it and whoever will lose his life, for my sake, shall find it."

The new piety of peace of mind and soul, in spite of the fact that it is helping many people to adjust themselves better to life and to the world as it is, must also come to terms with that aspect of religion which is concerned with man's efforts to transform himself and the world in the direction of what ought to be.

A gospel of smooth adjustment to the world as it is, with all its mediocrity and evil, leaves out that austere side of religious experience in which we see ourselves as pilgrims and pioneers, the creators of the colony of heaven in the wilderness of the world that is. The religious person at his best is never wholly content with himself and at peace with the world, for he knows how far he falls short of what he ought to be and can be. There is a positive and healthy tension between what is and what ought to be that forbids complacency and incites to action. We are admonished by St. Paul not to be conformed to this world, but to be transformed by the renewing of our minds that we may prove what is the good and acceptable and perfect will of God.

In so far as the new piety of peace of mind and soul permits us to forget or ignore the transforming task of religion, it is failing to offer a revival of individual conscience and ethical social concern. Remove these elements from religion, and what is left is a palliative, a painkiller, but not a healer and a restorer of courage and strength. The stern lesson of religion through the ages is: no peace of mind without adventurous thought and faith; no comfort without bold commitment to something better than the world that is; no abiding joy and security without loyalty to the best.

A second form of the new piety is the patriotic type. The intensity of the struggle with communism in recent years has led many to believe that since Communism is dogmatically atheistic in its philosophy, those who are opposed to communism must be dogmatically theistic. From here it is not a long step to the point where we make belief in God a test of a proper hatred of communism. And from this point one proceeds quickly to the assumption that God is not the Father of all mankind but the peculiar protector of the chosen people against the rest of the world. By this process we reduce our idea of

God to the level of the fierce tribal deity of the early Old Testament. We make Him into "an angry man, hating half the world." He becomes a sort of Big Brother upon whom we call for aid in our struggle. We assume His sanction and aid for whatever we propose to do since He is on our side.

Now there are many sound reasons for opposing communism, and the person who today can see no differences of ethical value between the ways of communism and the ways of democracy has certainly lost his power to discriminate between relative good and evil; but the tendency to think of God as the Big Brother destroys a higher and nobler vision of God which has been one of the best contributions of Judaeo-Christian faith. God is not the guarantor of any particular nation's destinies. As the prophets of Israel—and Jesus after them—insisted, God stands for that power of truth and justice and righteousness and love before which all men and all nations are judged. The very foundation of an ethical view of the world is the realization that "God is no respecter of persons, but in every nation he that feareth him and worketh righteousness is accepted with him." We may trust that in our struggles we are on God's side. But it is presumptuous and untrue to insist that God must back us up whatever we do.

We do not become a better or more religious people because the name of God is engraved on our stamps and coinage, or even by adding the words "under God" to the pledge of allegiance to the flag. We shall not survive as a nation by trusting that God will be our ally in the conflict with our enemies. We become worthy to survive and to draw on the strength of God in the measure that our personal attitudes and our policies and actions as a nation genuinely reflect something of the divine justice, mercy, and love.

In so far as the new piety of patriotism permits us to forget this austere truth, it weakens our moral fiber as a people, degrades the idea of God, and points backward in time toward the primitive superstition and tribalism which the Hebrew prophets fought to overcome 2500 years ago. If we as a nation are truly under God, we will know ourselves as under the divine judgment, called to penitence and challenged to reveal in history a more universal justice, a wider compassion, and a more patient and long-suffering love than any nation has yet shown.

A third form of the new piety might be called the emotional shock treatment or surrender type. We live in anxious, desperate times, and nobody can blame us if we are hungry for a sense of assurance and certainty which we cannot find. The temptation is always upon us to escape from the severe disciplines of reason, from the effort to think things through to some sort of sensible conclusion, from the tensions of doubt and questioning, from the challenges which make faith an adventure involving risk and the possibility of failure. A piety of emotional shock offers a way out. It calls on us to abandon thought, to ridicule reason, to acknowledge the complete helplessness and incompetence of our minds, and by an act of desire and will to throw ourselves on the mercy of God and accept a scheme of supernatural salvation.

The prospect is in many ways alluring. No man who has attempted to think his way through the great problems of life can fail to regard with humility the vast gap between the reach of the human mind and the size of the mystery which surrounds and includes it. No one knows better than the thinker that reason is not enough, and that all human thought is at last defeated by the stubborn mysteries of life. But he can only reply that the abandonment of thought is not enough either. It would doubtless be a great relief to feel oneself "safe in the arms of Jesus." The vast crowds, the skillful modern techniques of presentation, the repetitive dogmatic assertions are emotionally stirring and satisfying. But the thoughtful religious person cannot get out of his head the great command which says: "Thou shalt love the Lord thy God with all thy heart and with all thy soul, and *with all thy mind . . .*"—the heart and soul and strength along with, not instead of, the mind.

While the piety of surrender may well induce a vigorous, positive response and even a deep desire to live a new life, it does not show much evidence as yet of aiding the growth of the whole person into an intelligent devotion to higher ethical and spiritual values, which is the only true revival of the religious spirit. In the midst of all the crowds, the floodlights, the techniques, the yelling and the general excitement, the earthquake, wind, and fire, a still, small voice whispers to the consciences of thoughtful men: "What doth the Lord require of thee but to do justly and to love mercy and to walk humbly with thy God?" And the words of Jesus set the standard of judgment: "By their fruits, ye shall know them."

The piety of patriotism, now in danger of losing itself in nationalism which is threatening to plunge the world into total war, must grow up until it dares confront us with a vision of God who is the God of all mankind and a humanity made up of many peoples and nations all precious in His sight. Any smaller idea of God simply dooms us to the tribal conflicts and hatreds from which we have been trying to escape for centuries.

The piety of peace of mind and soul must grow up until its priests and adherents dare present it as something more than psychotherapy with a religious tinge and smooth adjustment to the world as it is. Somehow it must arouse in men not only the longing for comfort and peace but a vision of themselves as they long to be and of the cleaner world they can help to make. Something of the ancient prophetic and apostolic fire needs to be rekindled in the piety of peace of mind, so that its adherents can move out of the vicious circle of their own neurotic fears and anxieties and seek their peace of mind in bold commitment to the effort to do something of God's will on earth.

The piety of emotional shock and surrender will have to face the fact that religion is something more—the steady, sober search for intellectual and emotional integrity, for wholeness and harmony of mind and heart, and for the expression of this wholeness in patient, intelligent effort to realize, in the world as it is, the best possible ethical ideals and policies.

If these changes can take place in the prevailing popular pieties, there is at least a chance that our age may indeed witness an authentic revival of the religious spirit which could save us and our children from the prospect of continual frustration and anxiety and the ever-present dread of total destruction.

Meantime, there is another evidence of the possible existence of a religious revival which seems to me both more general and more important than any of the prevailing popular pieties. There has been a slow and subtle change in the mood of thought and feeling with which people approach religion. This has been due to the collapse of certain illusions by which many people lived until quite recently. There were in the 1930's hosts of people whose interest in religion centered in it as a means to social and political reform. Their real faith was that social and political reforms were ends in themselves and that religion could be a powerful aid in bringing about the necessary changes.

One meets this attitude today far less often than one used to. It is not that the concern for social change has decreased. Rather the problem is now seen by many in larger dimensions. The reformation of society, the idea of the kingdom of God on earth, is seen to be not merely a matter of laws, commissions, organizations, and programs. It is also a matter of man's spiritual orientation, his knowledge of himself, his faith in his own powers, his feeling of belonging not only to the human community but to some deeper and more enduring community of faith and meaning which was before he was and will be after he is gone. There has been an unmistakable revival of interest in what we used to call "personal religion" as distinguished from "social religion" or "the social gospel." This revival is healthy in that it recognizes the roots of faith and hope from which all significant action springs and is a sincere search for a better understanding of those roots as they exist and influence the lives of individuals.

A second evidence seems to me to exist in the widespread abandonment of what might be called the negative dogmatisms. One meets some people today who are frankly cynical and many who are skeptical about religious faith. But there are few of these who are happy about it or proud of it. The smugness has gone out of cynicism and the skeptics are asking the questions which will lead at length to affirmation. One meets many agnostics but few atheists. The agnosticism is humble and open rather than self-satisfied. The agnostic of yesterday appears to have enjoyed his condition but the agnostic of today would like to be convinced. He knows that it is frivolous to confront the ultimate issues of life as if he were not really concerned with them. He does care about the meaning of life and he would like to know more.

Disillusioned with force, with politics, and with science as saviors, man today searches within himself for hints of those foundations of truth and justice and love on which his thought and action must be based if his power is to be put in the service of justice, his politics redeemed from triviality and corruption, his science devoted to the enrichment of life.

"Man," said Albert Schweitzer when he accepted the Nobel Prize for Peace, "has today become superman because of the power for good or evil which science has placed in his hands. But the superman suffers from a fatal imperfection in his spirit. He is not elevated to that level of superhuman reason which must correspond to the possession of superhuman force."

Perhaps the single greatest factor which makes for a genuine religious revival today is the fact that men everywhere are becoming aware of this terrible truth and are uneasy about it. It is in this uneasiness and restlessness that the search for higher values, the search for God, can begin. The most important need is: the reorientation of the human spirit so that man sees himself as a child of the Universal God, conceived in dignity and in freedom, sharing a common humanity with all men the world over, answerable to abiding values of truth, justice, and love, in the service of which he finds himself.

Two ■ No Peace of Mind

The pieties of peace of mind, of patriotism, and of shock and surrender have won large numbers of followers, and yet I would raise the question whether any one of them is profound enough and true enough to meet the real religious needs of modern man. They may be able to help assuage anxiety. They may make it somewhat easier to live in a swiftly changing and chaotic world. But they are at best approximations or substitutes for religion. And at worst they do downright harm by offering comfortable, exciting, or shallow half-truths in answer to the real fears, anxieties, and tragedies of our human condition.

It is all very well to say with Dr. Peale, "Change your thoughts and you can change anything." This is a half-truth. Your attitude towards any situation makes a great deal of difference, but it does not necessarily change the situation. A good part of life consists of the acceptance of situations which we did not make and cannot change. If we try to tell people that all things are possible if they will only think good thoughts, we lead them towards eventual disillusionment and frustration. For all things are not possible. We are what we are, and others are what they are, and the world is what it is. Human purposes and energies can change situations in some degree, but there will always be for all of us certain given conditions under which we must learn to live, certain human relationships which we must work out in the best possible way, certain tasks to be done whether we feel like it or not. People have often asked me how a minister manages to prepare and write a sermon each week. The answer is very simple. It is expected of you. It has to be done whether you feel like it or not, whether at the moment you are inspired or not, whether you feel religious or not. Our thoughts do change situations in a way. If I love my work, I will do it better and it will be a joy rather than a burden to me. But whether I like it or not—and I cannot like everything I have to do—I must still do it as cheerfully and competently as possible. Necessity and obligation form a very large part of life. Often they are the ties which bind us to sanity in time of stress. Difficult and heavy as our obligations may be, they carry with them a positive value. They give us the dignity of knowing that we are needed by someone or some cause or some great purpose, that we are of real value.

The present peace of mind cult seems to suggest that there is a way whereby people can be released from their anxieties entirely and attain complete happiness and freedom. I do not believe it. I do not even believe that it would be a good thing if it were possible. Anxiety and strain are part of normal life. It is true that when they become too intense they cripple us, but without anxiety we would be more seriously crippled. The positive sides of anxiety and fear are foresight and planning. We do not attempt the impossible because we see that it really is impossible. We approach difficult decisions and tasks only after we have thought through the best way of meeting them, calculated the risks involved, and decided that though dangerous they can be done. A fish is a beautifully adjusted creature. He swims with grace and ease and knows just how to behave in his watery environment. He is without anxiety. But remove him from the water, and he flops around helplessly and soon dies.

Man, on the other hand, is not so well adjusted in a physical sense. He cannot swim as well as a fish or run as fast as most of the four-legged animals or fly as well as a bird. Yet because of a certain restlessness, a curiosity, a sense of strain, a desire to know and experiment, man has managed to make his way across the earth and across the sea and into the air. Anxiety and strain are spurs which incite us to new discoveries which create new and better ways of life.

More profoundly, it may well be asked whether we have any right to peace of mind in a world like this, whether the proper religious goal is smooth adjustment to the world as it is. If peace of mind is simply a state of being undisturbed by the pressures of life, carefree, without anxiety, happy, well-adjusted, successful in a sick and tormented world, its moral significance would appear to be largely negative. Have we any right to be complacent and at peace in a world where men have developed the weapons wherewith to destroy civilization entirely, but neither the will nor the wit to control those weapons in the interests of human welfare? Who dares be at peace in a world where the privileged grimly refuse to share their privileges? Who dares be at peace in a world where millions are hungry and oppressed and ground down by poverty and disease? Who dares be at peace in a world where the poisons of racial hatred still run rampant? Who dares be at peace when he knows so well the grip which narrowness and meanness and greed and selfishness have on his own heart?

It is significant that the great religious figures stand out as great precisely because they were out of tune with their times. Their consciences were uneasy and troubled. Their messages were words of unrest designed to arouse the sluggish consciences of men to a kind of action which would change the world, overcome existing evils, break down the barriers which shut men off from one another. They were anxious men driven by a deep desire to change themselves and the world around them. They were passionate men who felt deeply about the evil which they saw and the need to do something about it. They were non-conformists who saw their mission not as adjustment to the ways of life which were popular and familiar, but as transformation and even destruction of those ways of life in order that better ways might be found and followed. Such peace of mind as they knew was not a quality of freedom from concern and anxiety but a realization that they had done their best to make a constructive solution to those problems possible. The way of peace of mind is to take up the burdens of concern and responsibility, to bear the yoke of love and sympathy and human concern, to face the tragedy of life with courage and confidence.

It is here that the peace of mind cult fails to help men realistically. This is a tragic world full of deep and unavoidable suffering, defeat, and failure. It is a world in the process of important and far-reaching change. In such a world, it is not enough to be immune to the pressures and challenges which surround us on every side. Indeed, if we actually succeed in immunizing ourselves we shall be unable to do the things which are necessary for survival. For what is required of us is not repetition of the mistakes of the past, perpetuation of the old ways of doing things, but a fresh start, a new approach to a whole cluster of new problems. If you are facing a wholly new and challenging situation you had better not have peace of mind about it. You had better be alert and ready to act, your mind searching for meaning, your energies ready to be used as soon as you see the direction you must take.

I profoundly hope and pray that our political leaders have no peace of mind about such desperately important issues as the prevention of war, the control of nuclear weapons, the protection of our traditional freedoms of speech and religious worship, the necessities of aid to the hungry and the oppressed. I hope they will not leave these matters to God or trust that they will all work out all right in the end. In this dangerous and tragic world, we simply cannot afford that kind of peace of mind, and if we achieve it we may well fail to survive as a nation.

The philosophy of the peace of mind cult today seems to be based on two principles, one psychological, one religious. It is a combination of elementary psychology and primitive religion. The psychological principle is best illustrated in the familiar children's story of "The

Little Engine That Could." You will recall that the big engine broke down at the foot of a steep grade, and there was only a little engine to take on the difficult task of hauling the train over the grade. But the little engine was not daunted even though everybody laughed at its small size and apparent weakness. It was coupled to the train, and it started off puffing to itself: "I think I can, I think I can, I think I can," and sure enough, the big train began to move, and the little engine that thought it could pulled it triumphantly over the grade. Of course, there is truth in this principle. No good thing can be done without self-confidence and the will to do it. But when you elevate this principle to a philosophy of life it becomes absurd. There are a great many things in this world which any given person simply cannot have or do, no matter how much he may want to, no matter how confidently he may think he can. If you tell a man that things are not really so bad as he supposes, that all the good things he desires he can have if he will only believe, you will increase his frustration and ensure his ultimate disillusionment.

A prominent clergyman has declared that our religious faith has been "resurfaced" and that, thanks to President Eisenhower, "prayer and righteousness" have been "popularized." Now it is fine that these things are so, if they are so, but the view of God which seems to be suggested is a very primitive one. He is a kindly old gentleman with a white beard who sits on a throne "up there" and listens to the prayers of his people "down here." He tries to see to it that we get what we want. Such a concept of God takes us back to the days before the great Hebrew prophets, when God was conceived as the protector of the chosen people against all other peoples, when he had his own favorites whom he supported not because they were more just and righteous than anyone else but because he liked them better. Perhaps the greatest step towards mature religion in all history was taken 2500 years ago when the great Hebrew prophets attacked this idea and proclaimed that God was the God of all men, that his will was justice, truth, righteousness, and peace, that all men would be judged equally on the basis of how truly they sought to reach these high standards, and that if there was a chosen people, it had been chosen not for special privilege but for special responsibility. The literature of the peace of mind cult leads one to accept not the universal God of all mankind but the God who is a cosmic errand boy for his favorites.

I must therefore raise the question whether the peace of mind cult is in the historic sense Christian in any sense of the word. Rather it seems to me to be pre-Christian and even pre-Judaic. It is a revival of an ancient superstition embellished with modern psychological jargon. And there is a further question: can this strange combination of primitive religion and modern psychology really produce the results which it claims to produce? Does evil really vanish if we refuse to recognize it? Will God, the God of righteousness and truth and justice, really step in and extricate us from the results of our own foolishness and malice? Is the achievement of the good life really a matter only of thinking that we are good long enough and hard enough? Whenever I consider the preaching of the peace of mind cult I wonder how one would present it to various groups of people in the world. Would one dare present it to starving people in India or China? Would one have the nerve to say to them: "Change your thoughts, and you can change anything"? Would one dare present it to those heroic Hungarians who after years of tyranny showed by terrible but brave and noble resistance to the tyrants that their spirits were not broken, who died by the thousands because they believed in freedom? I fear the words of this peace of mind gospel would stick in my throat if I tried to speak them to people like this. The suffering and agony of our world must be met by stronger stuff.

The people I have known who have seemed to me to possess real peace of mind are so absorbed in the tasks they have undertaken that they have hardly had time to ask themselves whether they possess peace of mind or not.

We all seek peace of mind. We all need it. It is one of life's most precious spiritual gifts, but it cannot be bought cheaply. It cannot be had at the price of a few superficial psychological maxims and the revival of some primitive religious ideas of God. Wordsworth wrote of "central peace subsisting at the heart of endless agitation." That is what we all seek: a quiet place within the mind and spirit where there is order and meaning and where the living waters of faith and courage flow. But we do not come to this place by trying to escape from the pressures and anxieties of life. We come there only as in the midst of "this endless agitation" we begin to discover that there are more resources of courage and endurance than we had supposed. The "peace of God which passes all understanding" comes not with much seeking but when we have ceased to seek it as an end in itself because we are occupied with the actual work of God in the world.

The high priests of the peace of mind cult have assured us that life is very simple. Their teaching is well-intentioned and superficially useful. But it is not profound enough or Christian enough or true enough to meet the real needs of men in a tragic and complicated world. The peace of mind gospel may lead to some new teaching—perhaps hypnotism or new tranquilizing drugs. But man's hunger and need for authentic peace of mind will not be assuaged.

Essential religion is not a prop or a tool for us to use in assuaging our griefs, solving our problems, and making things turn out well for us. Religion does sometimes bring these gifts, but they are gifts of grace, unearned and often undeserved. We seek religion because it is good in itself, true, worthy of our thought and service, essential to the peace and even the survival of mankind. Religion deals not only and not primarily with what is wanted by man but with what is demanded of man as a rational spiritual being, as a child of God. Its benefits to man are by-products of the search for the highest values.

There is more peace of mind in one honest and sincere effort to uphold the principle of freedom in the community, to speak out against the lie, to practice the ethics of brotherhood than in all the books and pamphlets in the peace of mind library.

Our forefathers may have been naive from our enlightened point of view, but they fought their spiritual battles on their knees in the presence of a God of justice and judgement and truth. They believed in him. They believed in themselves and in their own powers. They believed it was their right and even their duty to share with him the long task of making themselves and the world somewhat better than when they entered it. We fight our spiritual battles not on our knees but on psychiatrists' couches, in courses designed to relieve us of worry and strain, in group work situations, in public opinion surveys. Our forefathers knew that religion was not primarily medicine to soothe the weary soul but a force which drove them out to change themselves and the world. Such peace as they found was enough to make them vigorous, creative people, doing what they conceived to be the will of God on earth with all their might. They could pray: "Lord, teach us to regard not overmuch who is for us or against us but to see well to it that Thou be with us in everything we do." They were stern and stubborn, often mistaken, not always tolerant and kind, but perhaps they were closer to the truth than the modern, streamlined practitioners of religion who preach personal comfort and success.

The pieties of peace of mind, of patriotism, and of emotional catharsis are nothing new. They are merely a continuation of the palliatives which have failed in the past. They do not constitute a revival of religion but an unwillingness to face the real issues which religion poses, the real problems which it calls upon man to face. But there is in our day the possibility of a deeper and truer revival of religion. We could conceivably begin to think and feel religiously about some of the real issues: our deep need for a framework of meaning which is large enough to encompass the new discoveries in the expanding universe and the untold possibilities for human development; our crying necessity to find new paths in human relations so that the prejudices and fear of men no longer prevent them from the cooperation which can alone make peace possible; our hunger for better knowledge of ourselves and of others which can bring about the realization of the goals of brotherhood and love which have hitherto been "the impossible ideals" of the great religions of mankind.

Three What Kind of Religious Revival?

The most important question about the religious awakening which is being hailed on every side today is: What kind of religion is being awakened? For religion is a complex and many-sided expression of human needs, desires, fears, and hopes. Sometimes the dominant emotion in religion is fear. When it is, people use religion as a bulwark against possibilities which they dread and hate. Sometimes the dominant emotion is a narrow and self-centered desire. When it is, people use religion as a means to an end. They hope to gain something by it: success or security, popularity or privilege. Sometimes the dominant emotion is hope—the hope of a better kind of life, a life with more meaning, more usefulness, and more joy than life now holds. When hope is the dominant emotion, religion takes on a more positive and outgoing aspect. It becomes a quest, an adventure, a pilgrimage in the process of which people rediscover themselves and their fellow men and the world in wider perspectives. Sometimes the dominant emotion is love, and when it is, then people not only rediscover themselves and their world; they also transform themselves and their world. Hope in the religious sense is a vision of the better self and the better world that might exist. Love in the religious sense is the driving power whereby hope is in some measure realized in individual life and in the world as it is.

Is the present widely hailed religious revival driven by our fears and our narrow, self-centered desires, or is it the work of our hope and our love? The issue has been vividly stated in some lines by the Irish poet William Butler Yeats:

> We had fed the heart on fantasies,
> The heart's grown brutal from the fare;
> More substance in our enmities
> Than in our love*

The words are an indictment of our generation. In religion, as in our social and political life and our view of world affairs, there has been of late "more substance in our enmities than in our love." Therefore, in too many ways, the kind of religion which is being revived is not helping us to understand ourselves better, to deepen our feelings of brotherhood with all men, and to find new and ethical solutions to the vast problems which we face. Rather, its effect seems to be to confirm us in our hatreds, to sanctify us in our self-centeredness, and to justify thoughtlessness and ethical mediocrity.

But it is neither fair nor sensible merely to criticize the trivialities and absurdities which pass for a religious revival today. The simple truth is that the world is in desperate need of an awakening or reawakening of the religious spirit in all its beauty and variety and power. It is not too much to say that only the emergence of large numbers of people whose minds and spirits have been renewed by fresh visions of life's religious meanings and obligations can save us from the doom towards which we seem to be blindly and fatalistically stumbling today. One has a strange, uneasy feeling today that we go through the motions of life as if its very existence were not threatened. There is a tragic paradox in the fact that at the very moment when the healing science discovers a way to protect our children, and ultimately the world's children, against the scourge of infantile paralysis, power politics is grinding towards the time when no child can be safe and no home secure from our enmities and fears. The present awakening of popular interest in religion has

* William Butler Yeats, "The Stare's Nest by My Window," *Collected Poems,* The Macmillan Co., New York, 1956.

as yet offered us no hope, no way, no spirit of courage and faith with which to meet this scourge, though it is a thousand times more dangerous to us all than any disease. Rather, it seems to urge us to go on, as in a dream, assuaging our fears by a fatuous faith that somehow God will make it turn out all right for us. We rest complacently in the illusion that a little more piety and good intentions will prove enough. Yet piety and good intentions are not enough.

An authentic revival of the religious spirit within and among us will search us to the depths. "It is a terrible thing to fall into the hands of the living God." If and when such a thing happens, we shall be different, not only in our social and marital adjustments and our attitudes towards our jobs, but in our whole way of life: in our art, our literature, our politics, our economics, our attitudes towards other races and religions, and even, one hopes, in our foreign policy.

The first change which a genuine religious awakening will bring is the reversal of Yeats' lines. There will begin to be more substance in our loves than in our enmities. The mood of our spirits will shift. We shall discover what has been called "the expulsive power of a new affection." Personally we are made whole and healthy as we learn to live, not by what we hate and fear but by what we love and believe in. We break the power of what is evil and destructive within ourselves by letting loose what is good and creative. The dark and ugly impulses which all of us know in some measure lose their power over us as we become increasingly concerned with the fulfillment of that inward light and beauty which is also part of our being. As we learn to lead, as it were, from our strength rather than from our weakness, from our hope rather than from our fear, we find new possibilities in ourselves, in others, and in the whole world. In the wider sphere of our national and international life this change will be felt in the slow shift in emphasis and policy from the fear of communism to the active love of freedom, from the effort to contain the totalitarian revolution to the effort to promote the positive revolution of freedom and brotherhood, from retaliation to reconciliation. The Quaker, George Fox, expressed this necessary change, which is at the heart of all authentic religion, in these sentences:

> I saw that there was an ocean of darkness and death, but an infinite ocean of light and love which flowed over the ocean of darkness. In this I saw the infinite love of God and I had great openings.*

A genuine religious awakening, as it destroys the power of fear and self-centeredness within the spirit of man, will liberate him into a new kind of religious experience: the unmercenary love of the good. The tacit assumption of our acquisitive society in religion as in everything else has been the commercial one. We ought to get something out of it. We support it if we do; we are not interested if we don't. There is something more than a little blasphemous and sickening in the following analysis, from *Publishers' Weekly,* of the reasons for the boom in the religious book trade:

> Predicting that sales will be up in 1955, Broadman Press bases its optimism on the "continuing increase in the popularity of religious books, the heightening world tensions which cause more people to seek help through religion." †

One is tempted to paraphrase St. Paul and inquire if the book trade wishes the world to continue in tension that sales may abound. Religion at its deepest and best has a certain uncalculating quality. We seek the good because it is good; the true because it is true; the beautiful because it is beautiful. God is to be loved, not from hope of heaven here or hereafter, nor from fear of hell, here or hereafter, but because God is worthy of love. A genuine religious awakening among us will involve the seeking of the highest religious values without ulterior motives. It is a sad commentary on the superficiality of much contemporary religion that it has to be sold to the

* George Fox, *Journal,* Everyman's Library, J. M. Dent & Sons Ltd., London, 1924, p. 11.

† *Publishers' Weekly,* February 26, 1955.

public as a commodity which must compete on the open market with refrigerators, automobiles, and a million other useful gadgets. "Worship in comfort," reads a sign on a church. "This church is air-conditioned." Sadly it must be admitted that the scientist often reveals today the spiritual quality of unmercenary love for the truth far better than the churches reveal the unmercenary love of goodness. The good is to be loved for itself alone because it is at the heart of things.

A religious awakening will also be an awakening of thought, of the rational faculty in man. It will renew modern man's waning confidence in the power of the human mind to think its way towards truth. In this respect there is today some cause for optimism. The first half of the twentieth century did see a serious and profound rethinking of basic religious issues: of the idea of God and of human nature, of the mystery of good and evil, and of the relevance of the great Christian themes of suffering, tragedy, and redemption. It is safe to say that thinkers like Reinhold Niebuhr, Paul Tillich, and Albert Schweitzer are bringing about changes in man's thinking about religion which will have effects for generations to come. They have helped rescue religion from the intellectual doghouse by bringing to their studies of it not only a profound traditional knowledge, but an intelligent and broad knowledge of historical, psychological, scientific, and sociological thought. They have destroyed the rational foundations both for the too optimistic liberalism and for the traditional dogmatism of the last century. They have laid the foundations for a view of religion which sees it not as a specialized compartment of human life and activity but as a deeper and more meaningful way of understanding and sharing in all human activities and experiences. Not, I think, since the age of the Renaissance has there been as important intellectual activity in regard to religious questions as there is today. The average man today who takes the time and trouble to explore what theologians are trying to say will find that theology no longer deals with such questions as how many angels can stand on the head of a pin, but with the momentous issues of human existence: man's desperate struggle for faith and intellectual integrity, his knowledge of himself as both animal and child of God; his growing realization of both the limits and the vast possibilities within his mind and spirit. Not only theologians and philosophers, but ordinary intelligent people in any walk of life are beginning to think hard about the basic religious problems. I have recently had one of those revelations of the obvious which make one say to oneself: "You fool, why didn't you see that years ago?" I have found that people are intensely interested in religion. Close to the surface of many of us are the wonder, the terror, the hunger to know and understand, the desire to be better than we are, which have been everywhere the perennial themes of the world's religions. One of the few positive signs that a genuine awakening of the religious spirit may actually be in process today is the widespread willingness on the part of many people to wonder and think and talk about the great religious themes which formerly they either dismissed with indifference or solved with a trivial and superficial dogma. This pregnant wondering of modern man places him on the other side of dogmatism, cynicism, and indifference. It may be the beginning of a new age of reason and faith in which these two ancient antagonists will become allies and friends.

A genuine religious awakening will show itself in a revival of interest in the contemplative side of the religious life, not as a substitute for the active, ethical side, but as a guide and balance to its demands. For millions of people life, even religious life, has degenerated into mere activity, the busyness of one thing after another with no time or opportunity to reflect quietly upon the meaning of what is being done. Sometimes in the midst of organizations, committees, programs, and projects of a modern liberal church, the incessant edifying discussion and friendly sociability, one pauses wearily to wonder whether we really need all this for our religious growth; whether, indeed, our very earnestness in good works does not rob us of the collectedness and calmness which enable us to see life truly and see it whole. It may well be that a genuine religious awakening will result, not in more active churches, but in quieter churches; in more opportunities for people to "be still and know," rather than to analyze and discuss. At any rate, it seems certain that a genuine revival of religion will involve a rediscovery of the ancient religious practices of prayer, of meditation, of quiet openness to the winds of the spirit. If religion is not a utilitarian gadget or a drug to quiet the nerves and induce sleep but the realm of what is most real and important in life, then surely modern man's rediscovery of it will have to contain fresh ways of self-examination, meditation, contemplation, and prayer. For how are we to know what is most real and important and to apply it to our lives unless we take time to think about it and are willing to expend some energy on learning what it means to us personally? Prayer is not a method of getting what we want, as some of its modern advocates would have us think, nor is it a matter of wanting what we get, as the apostles of psychological adjustment are apt to tell us. It is a way over which the whole person, with all the powers of body and mind, feeling and desire, hope and purpose, moves towards some kind of living unity with the ground of Being, i.e., with God. He is not the "Man Upstairs" of whom we ask favors. He is that abyss of mystery and meaning beneath our life and all life out of which meaning and courage and love well up through men into the world. My beloved teacher, Willard Sperry, used to speak often of what he called "the reticence of God." All the words that have been spoken and written about him do not describe him. They are symbols and metaphors only. It is possible to live for months and years, perhaps even a lifetime, with no awareness of his presence and reality. It is likely that we shall do just this if we never take time to think and seek, to be still, and to wait openly. Nothing can be very real to you if you dismiss it with a cliché or bother to think about it only when you have nothing else to do. But those who have taken the trouble to pay more than casual attention to the search for God persist in telling us that He is, and that in Him they have found strength and vision and love. It is not likely that a religious awakening will provide us with any more exact description of the infinite mystery than this. What it will do is recall us from frantic haste and activity and teach us to leave behind both trivial denials and dogmatic descriptions and become humble and open before the presence of the divine mystery and love.

A genuine religious awakening will show itself in a new spirit of tolerance and brotherhood, a glad acceptance of the infinite variety of men and their insights into what is true and good and beautiful. The terrible outbreaks of cruelty, persecution, and inhumanity which our generation has seen have come from individuals and from whole societies which have lost or are losing their spiritual moorings. People who are really sure of themselves, who have come to some deep and humble convictions as to what life means and what is truest and best, feel no urge to be intolerant and to persecute the unbelievers. Why should they? Understanding something of the size and complexity of the infinite mystery, they expect and welcome varieties of thoughts and experiences about it. Who are they, after all, to make the preposterous claim that their own particular definitions and ways of life are the only true ones? The urge to persecute comes to those who are most insecure about what they themselves believe and who must, therefore, bolster up their weak defenses by compelling others to agree with them. Surely a genuine religious awakening will liberate men from fear of the stranger, the non-conformist, the person or the society that is different. The secret of human brotherhood is not that we shall come at last to be all alike: thinking, working, praying, building our societies all in the same way and with the same materials. The secret lies in the acceptance of the wonderful diversity of human insights, skills, and purposes—and in finding the creative ways whereby men can teach and learn from one another. The beauty of the tapestry is not in the color or texture of a single thread, no matter how unique and important that single thread may be. It is in the way the single thread is woven in with thousands upon thousands of other threads, each unique in itself, yet each a part of the pattern of the whole. A revival of the religious spirit will enable us to look with gladness and thankfulness at the threads of faith and meaning in our own household of faith and in all the great religions and civilizations of mankind, renouncing the absurd demand that they become like us and rejoicing in the wonderful richness of human diversity. It will create a spirit which lifts us above sectarianism and partisanship, out of the bog of nationalism and the clash of creeds and systems and enables us for the first time really to envisage the community of man.

I will not venture to predict that such a religious awakening as this is in the making today, here or anywhere else in the world. I hope it is, for the world needs it very badly. I hope it will come soon and swiftly, for the destructive forces are moving fast and furiously. It may be that their momentum is so great that they cannot now be stopped and that the revival will have to come out of the shattered remnants of our world or on some other and unknown planet.

But, for what comfort and reassurance it may give, there remains this possibility: I have written nothing of this needed revival of the religious spirit which is not stirring in millions of human minds and hearts the world over. The choices of life and death, of good and evil, of human grandeur or unspeakable degradation, the choices, as well as the faults, are, as Shakespeare reminded us long ago, "not in our stars, but in ourselves."

Four Your Doubts Are Important

I know a man with whom I served on a board of directors for a charitable institution. He was a chronic doubter. Whenever any new proposal was made, you could be sure that he would be the first to attack it with a whole string of questions and doubts as to its advisability, practicality, and usefulness to the work of the institution. Again and again I have watched this man throw his doubts around the meeting, irritating and challenging the proponents of the new idea. Meetings were often unduly prolonged, tempers lost, and unkind words spoken because this man persisted in his doubts. It was a long time before I realized that, annoying as he often was, this man was performing a very useful service for the institution. No idea was ever adopted until it had been subjected to every possible test. All the possible dangers had been faced and some way of meeting them discussed. Questions had been raised which forced the proponents of the idea to revise their thinking in the light of some of the objections which had been raised by the doubter. Sometimes his doubts were farfetched and could be safely ignored. But sometimes they touched an aspect of the matter which nobody else had foreseen. And when we were all through we usually had a sounder plan than we would have had if this doubter had not been present and articulate.

The religious awakening we need may well begin not in a great wave of reborn faith but in a great wave of doubt. Doubt at first glance seems to be a negative factor which fills our lives with uncertainty and anxiety. And it is surely true that we cannot live effectively if our minds contain nothing but doubt. But doubt also has its positive uses. It is a necessary condition of learning. If we cannot doubt, we cannot expand our ideas and our understanding. If we dare not question what is asserted by our fellow men to be beyond question, we cannot hope to discover any new truth at all.

The remedy for anxiety is not freedom from doubts and uncertainty. Rather it is the acceptance of doubt for the creation of wider knowledge and understanding.

Scientific progress, of course, is founded upon systematic, rational doubts. It was because men like Copernicus, Bruno, Galileo and others dared to doubt the truth of the ancient Ptolemaic astronomy that they were able to grasp a new view of the universe which placed the sun rather than the earth at its center and opened the way for modern astronomy. Because doctors have persistently doubted various traditional remedies for disease, they have been able to open the way to new and more effective remedies. In science doubt is not only a virtue, it is a way of life—and an essential. When two scientific theories are found to be in conflict with one another, this is not regarded as a disaster but as an opportunity. It means that there must be some facts in the situation which have not yet been discovered or, if they are known, have not been properly interpreted. It means that scientists must take a fresh look at the whole situation and probably expect to form a new theory which will be different and more comprehensive than either of the first two. Their doubts, questionings, and conflicts of opinion open the way to new knowledge and understanding.

This kind of doubt operates positively in the field of religion, too. The great prophets of Israel had to doubt the idea of the primitive tribal God of the early Old Testament in order to reach the profounder insight into the nature of the one universal God of all mankind. Jesus had to doubt the validity of the old moral law of retributive justice, "an eye for an eye and a tooth for a tooth," in order to reach the notion of a God whose attributes were not only justice but mercy, not only punishment but forgiveness. We ought, therefore, in thinking about religion, to pay attention to our doubts and uncertainties. They will mark the areas where we need to grow and can grow. Actually, there is no final certainty in our life any more than there is any absolute peace of mind. Every man's condition is summed up in a remarkable story from the Gospel of Mark (9:14-29). A father brings his son who is possessed by an evil spirit into the presence of Jesus. He says that the son suffers sorely from this illness and that the disciples of Jesus can do nothing to help. He asks if Jesus can help, and Jesus replies: "If you can believe, all things are possible to him who believes." And then this father replies with some words which have been in the minds of millions in the generations since. "Lord, I believe. Help my unbelief."

In every situation, we do feel doubt, we do have questions. If we postpone our action in any area until the time when we shall have absolute certainty we shall never act at all. The couple who are about to marry will never be able to do it if they insist upon being assured in advance that each will be the perfect mate for the other and that their marriage will be an ideal one. The young man who faces a choice among several jobs cannot afford to wait for the certainty that one will be the absolute best. He can only think hard, accept his doubts as inevitable in any situation involving choice, use his best judgement, and go ahead. The statesman who faces a complicated decision in international affairs cannot afford to wait until he has all the information he might want in order to make a right decision. He must use heart and mind and conscience plus all the facts he can get and then make his choice as an act of faith, carrying the burden of his doubts along with him.

Unfortunately, in these days the anxieties and fears of the time have created in millions of us an understandable hunger for certainty. But the widespread presence of this hunger often compels the man in a place of responsibility to pretend to a certainty which he does not feel. He dares not share his doubts and questionings, for this will undermine his influence with a great many people. In all important matters he must assume that he is absolutely right while all others are at least misguided if not malicious. If he reveals his own humanity, if he permits anyone save his closest advisors to know that he does have serious doubts and many unanswered questions, he destroys himself as the symbol of authority and certainty which most people want him to be.

Yet in perpetuating the fiction that those in authority can have no doubts a very important democratic value is lost. The ferment of ideas, the constant give and take of suggestions and opinions between the people and their leaders, is cut down to the point where only a few eccentrics and rugged individualists make themselves heard. A great many people abandon the difficult task of thinking for themselves and expressing their thoughts. The "great white father" is there. He knows best. He will decide. The hunger for certainty, the fear of doubt, the desire for some person in authority who will take from our weary minds the burdens of thinking for ourselves: these impulses in the age of anxiety are among the strongest ones making for dictatorship. Dictatorship is the way of people whose minds are tired and who would rather let somebody else decide their destinies for them. They long to "escape from freedom" because freedom puts such a heavy load of responsibility upon them. "The greatest danger to democracy," wrote the late Justice Brandeis, "is an inert people."

Not only in affairs of state is this hunger for certainty apparent. It also appears in the individual attitudes of persons in mental or emotional trouble or confusion. The minister, the psychiatrist, the psychological counselor all know the persons who come with long tales of perplexity and confusion and literally beg to be given an authoritative answer, a prescription, a simple solution to their problems. It is one of the primary disciplines of the responsible counselor to know that he must not give such an answer even if he thinks he sees one. The counselor will be doing the individual no real service if he does. Rather, he will be adding to the patient's craving for dependence on external authority, and crippling further his capacity to think freely and responsibly about the situation in which he finds himself. It is the constant temptation of anyone whose task it is to deal with the troubles of other people on a confidential basis to "play God." And it is a temptation which must be constantly resisted not only for the good of the person who is tempted but also for the good of those whom he is trying to help. To refuse to play God is the ultimate act of faith in the dignity and worth of other people.

Most people, as age and experience increase, learn to accept their doubts as more or less normal, if bothersome, parts of existence in a changing and precarious world. But in the field of religion we have been conditioned to expect certainty. Religious beliefs are usually presented as insights into reality which come not out of the constant ebb and flow of human experience but from some other realm by means of revelation. Revelation, it is argued, provides knowledge of a different sort from the ordinary knowledge which comes to us through experience and the reflections of the rational mind upon experience. The truth of revelation is not subject to the kind of criticism and questioning and doubt to which we submit all human claims to knowledge. It is arbitrary, beyond doubt, beyond logic. If it does not make sense to our minds, the fault is with our minds, not with that which is revealed. Indeed, one early church father, Tertullian, even went so far as to say that he accepted and believed the Christian faith precisely because it did not make sense to his mind. *Certa est, quia impossible est.* It is certain because it is impossible. One reaches certainty and peace only by the leap of faith.

Yet this leap of faith has proved increasingly hard for more and more people in our time. Trained in the sciences or the humanities, they want to see things whole. They cannot believe that what is true in one area of human knowledge and experience can be denied by the insights and experience from some other area. They resist the idea of the "department store mind," where varied ideas are carefully arranged on separate floors, with little communication between the department of religion and the department of science, between business or family life. If you want religion, you get off at the right floor, and there it is. But don't expect to find it on any other floor any more than you would expect to find men's suits in the toy department of Macy's.

But many people today are convinced that nothing that is true can be contrary to the spirit of religion. And therefore they dare to doubt even the claims of revelation when they go contrary to the best fruits of human thought and experience. One of the first of these great doubters is the subject of the profoundest book of the Old Testament, the Book of Job. Job suffered just about everything that it is possible for a man to suffer. In a series of disasters he was deprived of his wealth, his home, his family, and his health. His friends who came to comfort him insisted that this was the work of God and that the reason must be that Job had committed some grievous sin for which he was now being punished. But Job contended that he had always walked uprightly, done justly by his family and neighbors, maintained faith in God, and tried to walk in his ways. He dared to question and to doubt the wisdom and justice of God in his own case. He raised the questions of the problem of evil and undeserved suffering with which the minds of thoughtful men have been wrestling ever since. "If God is all-powerful, how can he be all good when he permits such unjust sufferings to fall upon the righteous? And if God is all good, how can he be all-powerful, for if he were he would not permit such things to take place?" Doggedly, Job persisted in his contention that while he believed in God he did not understand his ways and even dared to doubt his justice. "Though he slay me," cried Job, "yet I will trust in him. But I will maintain my own ways before him." At last, Job was forced to acknowledge that he could not comprehend the meaning of his suffering, that it seemed to be simply part of the human condition which had to be accepted. He reaffirmed his faith in God and humbly admitted that

God's wisdom and judgement were unsearchable. But his faith did not dispel his doubts. Rather it included them, accepted them, and made them part of his total attitude towards life and its meaning. By frankly expressing his doubts and carrying them along with his profound faith in God, Job achieved humility and maintained the integrity of his own mind. He became a symbol of the tormented man of faith, unwilling to accept glib and easy answers, daring to believe that life did have meaning, even though his limited human mind could not fully grasp it. Such a faith has the ring of truth and realism. It does not have to pretend that life is simple and that its mysteries and tragedies can be explained away by facile moralisms. There used to be a popular song called "Say It Isn't So." It is a nice song, but it is no answer to the tragic realities of our world. A faith that can stand up in such a world must face its dark realities as Job did and still be able to affirm a positive meaning at the heart of life. For millions of thoughtful men and women nothing less will do.

The answers to Job's questions have not yet been found and agreed upon. His predicament is familiar to us all in our moments of deep suffering and loss. "Why did this have to happen to me?" we ask. "What have I done to deserve the suffering which has come to me?" The persistence of these questions in our human life suggests something most important about the nature of all religious faith. It is not possession of final certainty and security. It is man's affirmation of a meaning which he does not fully understand. It is faith which accepts doubt, which accepts uncertainty, which recognizes the limitations of the human mind. It arises out of the discovery that in order to live at all a man must have faith in something: in himself, in other people, in some eternal meaning of which he is a part and to which he is related. He must hold this faith and grow with it no matter what doubts assail him, since without it he cannot live at all.

It is significant that even the greatest men of faith knew their periods of dreadful doubt and dark despair. Jesus of Nazareth cried out, "My God, my God, why hast thou forsaken me." I believe it was a real doubt which must have assailed him in that moment of agony; and far from decreasing his stature in our eyes, the fact that he doubted should enhance the magnificence of the faith which he affirmed along with and above his doubt, and should bring him nearer to each one of us as a human being. The great mystical thinkers of the Christian tradition speak of a state of being which they call "the dark night of the soul." It is a time when all the certainties have been stripped from them, when they feel a kind of cosmic loneliness and alienation from God and from their fellowmen. It is described by St. John of the Cross in these words:

> For truly in her dark night the soul feels the shadow of death and the groans and tortures of hell, as if she saw them bodily before her, for hell to her consists in feeling herself forsaken of God, and chastised and flung aside, and that He is outraged and wrathful. All this she suffers now; and, furthermore, she is overcome by a direful terror that it is forever. And she is haunted by this same sense of being forsaken and despised of all created people and things, particularly of her friends. She feels within herself a profound void and utter dearth of the three kinds of wealth which are ordered for her enjoyment, which are: temporal, physical and spiritual; and she sees herself plunged into the contrary evils, to wit: miserable trifles of imperfections, aridnesses, and emptinesses of the perceptions of the faculties and desolation of the spirit in darkness. To this is added that she cannot, owing to the solitude and desolation this night produces in her, find comfort or support in any teaching or in any spiritual master.*

Here speaks one of Christianity's saints and a man of great disciplined faith. Hundreds of others of equally great faith will bear witness to having had the same kind of experience. The men of great faith also bear witness to another truth. They did come through the dark night of the soul and emerge into faith again, not to be

* *The Dark Night of the Soul,* tr. by Gabriela Cunningham Graham Watkins.

freed forever from their doubts and questions but refined and strengthened by the suffering and soul-searching which their doubts had compelled them to undertake.

All of us experience, in greater or lesser degree, our own dark nights of the soul. Of course they are agonizing, discouraging, and they are seemingly endless. But most of us survive them, and there are some practical ways in which we can deal creatively with these periods of doubt and despair.

A weeping woman sat in my office. She had just lost by death her beloved husband, and she said she felt utterly alone and forsaken and helpless. "I ought to have faith," she said, "and I thought I did have faith, but now even that is gone. What shall I do?" Together we came not to a conclusion, but to a way of living. She was to try to have faith "sufficient unto the day." For the moment she was not to try to solve the vast question of why this sorrow had come to her but simply accept the fact that it had come and must be lived through. She was not to attack the mysteries of the meaning of death and the possibility of life after death. She was to seek the strength and courage and faith to meet the demands which were immediately before her. She was to put off until tomorrow anything that could be put off today and move forward slowly and steadily, believing only that what she must do she could do and what she must endure she could endure. In this way her genuine and profound grief would have time to do its constructive therapy of clarification and purification. Her dark night would end, not forever, but for long enough to let her get started again and be ready for the darkness when next it comes. In this process no doubts have been driven away for all time, no absolute certainties established. What has been done is perhaps both more important and more practical. A human being has faced the wildness and tragedy of the world, accepted it for what it is and herself for what she is, and seen the problem truly: not the removal of that wildness and tragedy but the discovery of ways in which one can live courageously, usefully, even happily in the very midst of it.

When the dark night of the soul is upon us our minds are not at their best, not fully alive, sensitive and creative, ready to deal with the profoundest questions of human life as adequately as the human mind can ever deal with them. Therefore it is often best to go on with some very simple tasks that need to be done. We cannot always be solving the riddles of the universe. In the deepest kind of darkness and doubt it is sometimes best to do nothing at all directly but rather some simple, well loved things which bring absorption of your interests, a challenge to your skills and even solace and joy.

I know a psychiatrist who, when he is troubled and tired, plays a hard game of tennis and says that some of his fastest and hardest shots on the court would otherwise have been directed against his patients. A steep slope to climb which uses all your wind and all your muscles can purge you of much despair and personal animosity and make doubt bearable and even creative. Pictures or music or books which affirm the hunger for creation in the artist and also in the observer or hearer or reader can restore the soul.

Sometimes the best thing to do in time of perplexity and despair is to turn deliberately away from your own troubles and see what you can do about the needs of others. Years ago as a student I remember a long session with one of my teachers in which I tried to lay before him my manifold confusions, doubts, and wonderings. They seemed very important to me, and I guess I was very much absorbed in myself. After we had talked a long time he said, "It might be good for you just now to go out and find somebody who is really in trouble and see what you can do about it." The words were like a shot in the arm. I had worked myself into that state of self-centeredness where I was really beginning to believe that I was unique in all creation, that nobody had ever suffered as I had. Once I began to look around at others I found that I was a quite ordinary person, suffering the pains of growth and immaturity like almost all the other students. As my capacity for sympathy and understanding with others began to grow, I found that my own problems could be seen in their proper perspective. They were real, but not unduly serious. They were difficult but not as difficult as those which many others were facing. They could be lived through. One could even grow because of them.

All these things can help you to keep your balance and your sanity, to maintain contact with the stream of ordinary life. Life does go on and you must go on with it. Your dark nights of doubt and perplexity can leave you wiser and stronger than you were before.

Your doubts may be the most important things about you. Doubt is the growing edge of religion as it is of all other knowledge. Dr. Billy Graham was once asked if he were ever troubled by doubts. He replied that he was, but that they did not bother him much because he "never entertained them." On the contrary, perhaps Dr. Graham should invite his doubts in for an evening and entertain them in cordial and thoughtful discussion. He might find that they were among his truest friends. In days like these we had better "entertain" our doubts.

Five Where Is Your Authority?

"She is a lovely girl," said the young man with deep feeling, "beautiful and intelligent. We have many things in common and we want very much to get married. But how can we be sure that we are right for each other? What if we are mistaken? Isn't there any way to know for certain?"

I thought of the lines from George Meredith's sonnet:

> Ah, what a dusty answer gets my soul
> When hot for certainties in this our life.*

I tried to suggest to him that all important human relationships are at bottom acts of faith which must be entered into with as much knowledge as we can get, but always with a certain spirit of trust and confidence and hope. I suggested that if he waited for the perfect mate, or the perfect job, or the perfect home, he would never make the decisions which would lead him to a mate, or a job, or a home. But it was useless. In his questioning there was an almost pathetic hunger for a certainty which this world does not afford. He wanted me to be the authority to confirm or veto his decision to marry. Cruelly perhaps, but with conviction, I refused.

America's new piety is essentially a return to several sources of arbitrary authority in the field of religion. We are asked to return to the Bible as the authoritative word of God. Or we are asked to accept the revelation of final truth as it is embodied in the creeds of the Protestant church or the infallible teachings of the Catholic church, or the laws of Moses to the people of Israel.

* George Meredith, Sonnet Number 50, *Modern Love.*

Or we are asked to equate religion with Americanism and to believe in effect that what is good for America is good for God. Or we are asked to accept the idea that "God will take care of us," that "Father knows best," that if we pray hard enough he will show us the way.

Every religious point of view is based upon some source of authority, some standard of judgement and truth which is more than the mere preference or whim of an individual. Judaism rests upon the law, as contained in the first five books of the Bible and delivered by God to Moses. The Moslem faith rests upon the Koran, as received from God and set down by the prophet Mohammed. The teachings of the Buddha as given to his disciples form the fundamental authority of Buddhism. Hinduism likewise has its sacred writings, and the followers of Confucius and Laotse can turn for authority to the recorded words of these sages. Christianity claims not only the authority of the sacred book and the law, but also the authority of the unique and complete revelation of God in the person of Jesus Christ. Some branches of Christianity place the ultimate authority in the Church as an institution, and the Catholic church attributes the final authority in matters of faith and morals to the Pope, the Vicar of Christ on earth.

There may be truth in all these appeals to external authority, and yet one is compelled to raise the question of what happens to the millions of Americans of a scientific and experimental turn of mind. Can they accept this kind of authority, and should they? America grew strong and great precisely because her people relentlessly questioned the old foundations of authority from the divine right of kings to the arbitrary claims of the monolithic state as they have appeared in the twentieth century in both fascism and communism. Our peculiar vitality as a people has come from our propensity for asking questions, trying new ways, forsaking old doctrines when they did not serve our needs, formulating new beliefs on the basis of new experience. Can such a people really find relief from their deep anxieties by returning to old sources of authority which in most cases they long ago considered and abandoned? I think not.

When one first turns away from the external sources of authority and begins to drink the heady wine of freedom in religion, one is tempted to carry one's rebellion all the way. Released from the shackles of external and arbitrary authority, it seems for a while as if one were answerable only to one's own thoughts, desires, and preferences. But it is not really so. It is like the growing child in his mid-teens. He revolts, if he is healthy, against the authority of parents and of customs in the home, indeed against many adult sources of authority. His revolt is usually successful in most respects, and it is necessary to his growth into maturity and responsibility. But the revolt does not release him from authority. It merely exchanges some types of authority for others. For the customs of the home he substitutes conformity to the customs of his own group of contemporaries. For the authority through which "Mother knows best" or "Father says yes or no," he comes face to face with the necessity of reposing confidence in the authority of thought, judgement, and knowledge.

It is the same in religion. The way of freedom does not mean the absence of authority. Rather, it means the recognition and acceptance of certain new and living standards of authority which do not deny but fulfill the free mind, placing upon it new responsibilities and challenges. Every forward step in freedom is a step into new responsibility. When we leave behind the authority of parent or home or school, we move into the responsibility of making judgements and decisions for ourselves. When we leave behind the arbitrary authority of sacred book or creed or revelation or church, we move out into the responsibility of thinking for ourselves. Our freedom is greater in each case, but our burdens are greater, too.

The free man heeds the authority which comes from knowledge. In a small New England town on the morning of a great and destructive hurricane an old fisherman sitting on the pier took his pipe out of his mouth, sniffed the air, gazed at the sea and the murky sky, and said: "There's going to be a big blow. Better see that the boats are made fast." Immediately a whole series of events began to take place. Messages were sent over the phone and over the grapevine. Yachtsmen in their offices left the city early to make sure their boats were safe. When the full force of the hurricane struck in the late afternoon the fishing boats and yachts in the harbor were ready for it. They rode it out bravely and not a boat was lost.

Whence came this authority in the words of an old fisherman that bankers and lawyers, doctors and professors as well as his own fisherman colleagues listened with respect to his prophecy and obeyed his commands? It came from the knowledge and experience gathered from a lifetime of careful watching of the sea and the sky and the way the winds behaved. It came from the experience of many people that when that old man had a comment on the weather you took it seriously because it usually proved to be right. His was the authority of knowledge and experience.

We listen with respect and interest to the views of the person who knows whereof he speaks, who has a wholesome respect for facts and for the truth.

We attach authority to those new ideas and proposals which seem to fit in with familiar ideas which we believe to be true because they have been tested and found valid. Claims of arbitrary authority and absolute knowledge do not impress us. Is there any such thing as complete and final knowledge? Probably not, yet we do believe that the human mind is capable of knowing enough of truth to be able to make intelligent and informed judgements. And we honor the pursuit of knowledge as one of the most important human concerns. Certainly knowledge is a source of authority for the free mind, and reason is another. We ask of any proposition not only whether it is true, but also whether it fits in with the rest of the truth we know, and whether it makes sense. By reason we relate facts and truths to one another and shape them into patterns which lead to decision and action.

Man dreams of bringing the entire universe into some clear and orderly pattern of rational thought. The realization of this dream seems farther away today than it did several centuries ago, for our knowledge has grown faster than our reasoning powers. We have become aware of limits to human reason, of areas of life and experience which seem to be governed not by thought but by profound emotions and drives. Our generation has seen a retreat from reason, an explosion of human passions, fears, and hungers which so far defy the efforts of reason to control and direct them. Yet with all the limitations of reason we honor and respect it. At the least, we demand a rational justification for what we intend to do in any case. At the most, we soberly subject every idea and belief to the test of rational criticism. Truths and values that lie beyond the reach of the human reason do not block, but rather extend, the reach of the human mind. Thus, for example, no man can prove by reason the existence or nonexistence of God. But a man's reason may lead him to declare that God exists because in his view the truths which reason has revealed to him make more sense that way.

A third source of authority is practical utility. Does the idea or course of action work out well in actual practice? The libraries of the world are full of noble and persuasive arguments for all kinds of Utopias. The arguments for disarmament, or world government, or pacifism are logically unanswerable. These things are necessary. They are true. They are rational. But, as we have seen to our sorrow, between the idea and its fulfillment lie all the manifold obstacles and complications of the practical world, the age-old habits, prejudices, traditions, and inconsistencies of men and societies. The idea or course of action which is to win our respect and loyalty must be one which can prove its strength and durability in practice. There are dangers, of course, to the practical test. Not everything is good simply because it works. That which is practically successful must constantly be tested in the light of reason and knowledge. If men fail to do this, they become opportunists and devotees of what William James called "the bitch goddess, success." But, still, the free mind demands that its ideas live outside of the ivory tower.

A fourth source of authority for the free mind might be called the consensus of thoughtful people. We are suspicious of private revelations from on high. If anybody claims to have had one, we want him to tell us all about it and present it for criticism in the light of the experience of others. While we take pride in thinking for ourselves, we have learned from experience that no human mind, no matter how good it may be, can contain all facets of a complicated problem. The conference method of exploring ideas has become almost second nature to the free mind. When in doubt as to the right course, we turn to friends whose judgement we respect and listen carefully to what they say. For many years, the Quakers have practiced a technique for reaching group agreements which works remarkably well. They do not take votes on issues but, rather, work for what is called the sense of the meeting. If it is clear that the meeting is profoundly divided on a serious issue, action on that issue is postponed until further reflection has made compromise and ultimate agreement possible. The dangers of delay in this process are offset by the desire within each member of a group not merely to get his point of view accepted but to do his part in helping the group as a whole to reach a fair and sound position. The authority which the sense of the meeting carries is far greater than that which is carried by a decision arrived at through a close vote. It is dangerous, of course, to make the sense of the meeting the sole source of authority. Sometimes the majority is wrong, and a minority is right. But on the whole, even when that minority of one is right, it is better that his rightness be tested, examined, and confirmed by the consensus of thoughtful people. Knowledge, reason, practicality, and the consensus of thoughtful people—these four sources of authority are familiar to the free mind. They are in constant use in all sorts of human concerns and, while they do not possess and cannot claim the kind of absolute finality claimed for the Sacred Book, the

Law, the Creed, or the Pope, thoughtful people accept them and are willing to live by them.

But there are also two other sources of authority for the free mind, not so easily recognized but nevertheless powerful and important. One of them is intuition. Sometimes a reasonable proposition simply does not feel right. Overwhelming as the evidence for it seems to be, you do not like the idea. You have a hunch that there is something wrong. Such hunches are not unknown in science and have resulted in some remarkable discoveries. They appear constantly in the arts, and in the course of life we all know what it is to back our intuitions against the evidence and to discover that they did not betray us. No one quite knows how to describe what intuition is, but everyone has experienced it. It is the quick, sharp insight into a perplexing situation in which you know, perhaps after months of wondering and double-mindedness, what it is that must be done. It is the poet's capacity to grasp and state not only the facts but the feel of life as it is actually experienced. It is the saint's ability to see to the very heart of a problem and to grasp not only what a man is saying but what his desires, hopes, and fears are. We are, no doubt, properly suspicious of people who claim to live mainly by hunches and intuitions. They can be dangerous and destructive, and not every hunch we get is proved right. But the fact remains that, no matter how reasonable, practical, intellectually sound, and socially approved an idea may be, there is little that can be done about it if it does not have the consent of the heart.

The last of our six sources of authority is love. I am not thinking of love in the sentimental or romantic sense but of love as that force within life which makes for liberation from fear and anxiety, for the setting free of dammed-up emotions and unused energies, so that we use all our powers for some good end. It was said of Jesus that he taught as "one having authority, and not as the scribes." The authority seems to have consisted not in his knowledge, which was certainly no greater than that possessed by many of his contemporaries, nor in his reasoning ability or practical-mindedness, nor certainly in the support he received from thoughtful people, but in a kind of disinterested love. When he spoke, he spoke with love, that is, with the welfare of those to whom he spoke in mind. We are all sensitive to the presence or absence of this quality of love in all sorts of ways. We will listen to hard words from one who we are convinced truly loves us, words which would fill us with rage if they came from someone else. We will trust the man or the church or the government which has been able to convince us that its motivation is genuine concern for human welfare. We will trust it even when we disagree with it on certain specific points because we know it is sound at its foundations. None of the other foundations of authority carry much weight with us unless this one is also present, permeating all the others with the spirit of friendly concern and sympathy. But when this one is present we feel at home.

Here then are the sources of authority by which the free mind lives: Knowledge: Is it true? Reason: Does it make sense? Practicality: Will it work? The consensus of thoughtful people: How do others feel? Intuition: How do we ourselves really feel? Love: Is the motivation one of sympathetic concern? The way of freedom asks a hard thing. It asks us to think and feel our way into life's deepest meanings and truths without advance knowledge of what we will find. When I used to study algebra I had a book which had all the answers to the problems carefully arranged in the back. I thought this was a great help at first, but I soon got into the habit of looking up the answer before I started a problem and working backward from the answer to the problem. Consequently, I passed the course but never learned any algebra. The way of freedom does not give you the book with the answers on the last pages. It states the problems and the principles of authority by which thoughtful and sensitive people have worked their way through the book of life and found it both rewarding and beautiful.

Millions today are hungry for a way of life and a faith

which are their own discovery, not something handed down to them from the past. However weak or fitful or full of doubt and questioning their religious life may be, they want it to be a sincere quest, a genuine expression of what they really are. They do not wish to escape responsibility for themselves and for the world, but to undertake it. They are here not to run away from authority but to accept and follow the kind of authority which makes sense.

It is often asked what holds the people of freedom together, what enables them to work cooperatively when they acknowledge no fixed creed and no final and binding authorities except those which come out of the integrity of their own minds. The rule of liberal authority is that men in their search for truth shall use substantially the same methods and tests, shall respect facts, use reason, test ideas in action, consult frequently together, trust their deepest insights, and carry on the quest in the spirit of love towards one another. Their differences in opinion and belief will be a source of challenge to their minds and a means of growth in understanding and wisdom. The authority they will honor and obey will not be an external one imposed from without but an internal one created by their appreciation for the best that is within them and their respect for the best that is within others. The authority by which they live will be earned, not decreed; responsible, not arbitrary; flexible, not rigid; dynamic, not static. Only that kind of authority is good enough for people who have claimed the high privileges and profound responsibilities of freedom.

Six The Rediscovery of God

A popular song tells a good deal about the current rediscovery of God. "Have you talked to the Man Upstairs," it begins. Those who hear the melody on the jukeboxes are told that in time of trouble the Man Upstairs will see them through. It is enough to "say a simple prayer," and through the clouds will shine the face of the Man Upstairs. Sentimental, and in some ways repulsive, as the song is, it is significant as a symbol of our time. It stands for modern man's sense of spiritual loneliness.

It is really not surprising that man's first apprehensions of God should be expressed in very human terms and figures of speech. The God described and experienced by the early Old Testament writers is not very different from the "Man Upstairs" of the modern song. He guides and upholds his people when their ways are pleasing to him. He rewards them when they are good, and punishes them when they are bad. He walks in the garden in the cool of the evening and talks with Abraham as he sits at the door of his tent. He provides miracles and signs to prove his power on earth and his interest in the destinies of his people. He is pleased by flattery, disturbed by the impoliteness or indifference of his people, and he enjoys the savor of the meat which is roasted at the time of the sacrifice. He insists that men give visible proof of their devotion to him and even requires that a father be willing to sacrifice his own son as a demonstration of his fidelity. He is very human in his character, though superhuman in his power and knowledge.

The Bible is, in one sense, a biography of God. It shows

him first in this primitive human shape. But in the course of the nearly 2,000 years of human development which the successive books of the Bible reflect, God, so to speak, grows up and matures. With the great prophets he becomes the God, not only of Israel, but of all mankind. His concerns shift from ritual praise to ethical behavior. He cares less for "the blood of bullocks," and requires that men "do justly, love mercy and walk humbly" in his ways. Justice, Mercy, Truth, Love become his attributes. He manifests himself in the wonders and the orderliness of nature as Creator and Sustainer. In the human figure drawn from Jewish patriarchal family life, he appears as Father, the wise, loving, stern, yet tender, ruler and provider for the human family. He becomes identified with meanings and purposes which transcend and include the individual lives of men; he is that power and purpose in the world which will not rest until justice has been enthroned over all the earth.

In the New Testament he so loves the world that he gives his only-begotten son. Beneath the world's suffering and tragedy, he waits and yearns that his kingdom may come to birth. He is "a spirit, and they that worship him must worship him in spirit and in truth." He is that mysterious all-embracing spiritual reality "in whom we live and move and have our being." He is personal, yet more than a person. He is personal in the sense that men can feel a relationship with him, a loyalty to him, a love for him which is personal on their part and which is in some strange way reciprocated on his. He is a firm foundation of strength and confidence so that a man can pass through the struggles of life with courage and trust and even say, with St. Paul: "For we know that all things work together for good to them that love God." The depths of God's being are hidden in mystery so that a man can only say: "Eye hath not seen, ear hath not heard, neither have entered into the heart of man the things which God hath prepared." God comes at last in the Bible to stand for all the possibilities which surround human life, all the good as yet unrealized, all the beauty and truth as yet unknown. "Beloved, now are we the sons of God and it doth not yet appear what we shall be."

It should not be surprising that just as the idea of God in the centuries covered by the Bible undergoes a tremendous development and expansion, so also an individual's idea of God may develop and expand in the course of his own life and experience. The life of the individual does, or at least can, recapitulate the religious experience of the race. We all start with very primitive, literal ideas of God. We start with something like the "Man Upstairs."

Years ago, when I was a boy in school, I thought I knew very well what God was and what he looked like. He looked like Alfred E. Stearns, our headmaster: tall, erect, white-haired, the very essence of stern yet just and kindly authority. It seemed to me that God must rule the universe in much the same way that Alfred Stearns ruled the academy. And when, at Sunday vespers in the darkened chapel, while we students obediently bowed our heads, Alfred Stearns said: "Thou shalt love the Lord thy God with all thy heart, with all thy soul, with all thy mind, and with all thy strength; and thou shalt love thy neighbor as thyself," I was never quite sure who was speaking, God or Alfred Stearns.

No doubt this was superstitious, yet even today, when I hear or repeat those majestic words of the two great commandments, I feel the same sense of holiness, of majesty, and of beauty which I knew then. Alfred Stearns is dead, and I don't suppose I ever really believed that he was literally and personally God, but through him there entered into my consciousness something of the spiritual reality which is God. He was, so to speak, a channel through which the living spiritual waters flowed into the minds and spirits of many wondering and confused boys.

I suspect that all our religious experience begins at some such simple and anthropomorphic level as this. We were all children once, and some of us carry our childishness well on into adult life. We need not be ashamed of having once had, or indeed of still having, childish thoughts of

God. But there are two things of which we probably ought to be ashamed: One is persisting in our childishness throughout life. The other is supposing that because we have in a measure grown up and left behind our childish thoughts of God, there can be no other and deeper thoughts of God for the more mature and searching mind. When people begin for the first time to think seriously about God, it is almost inevitable that they will think in childish, immature ways. To know anything, we must begin at the beginning and grow up gradually through various levels of depth and meaning. We should not be surprised or upset if our own first thoughts about God begin at the simplest levels. Nor should we be religious snobs because we feel we have achieved a degree of maturity in our thinking, and brand as false or hypocritical those whose thought of God and need of God are now expressed at the simple level of the "Man Upstairs." The mark of maturity in the search for God is to keep on growing and searching.

The reappearance of the "Man Upstairs" idea of God in our time means that many people who have never bothered about God before are thinking about him for the first time. But the idea of the "Man Upstairs" is fortunately not the only phase of the current rediscovery of God. It takes a long time for a new vision of God to win the consent and acceptance of men. Jesus of Nazareth was rejected and crucified essentially because he sought to give simple and living expression to the idea of the universal God, the loving Father and Friend of all mankind which had been first interpreted by the great prophets of his people five hundred years before his time.

In somewhat the same way, a long-term reinterpretation of the idea of God may be reaching fuller and clearer expression in our own time after another period of nearly five hundred years. The idea of God as a separate being who created the world, established its natural and moral laws, and presided over it as ruler and judge, somewhat in the fashion of an oriental monarch, first began to be undermined in the theories of Copernicus and the observations of Galileo. Up until this time, the astronomy of Ptolemy had ruled the minds and speculations of men for a thousand years. The earth was the fixed center of the universe. The concentric domes of heaven arched over it. The deep pit of hell lay beneath it. The stars moved in their course across the dome of heaven, and above them were located in space the realms of the blessed. In the highest dome dwelt God himself. The Copernican astronomy changed all this in a very simple, but devastating, way. It presented the earth as a moving sphere and a single part of a much larger system. It removed the geographical locations not only of heaven and hell, but also of the dwelling place of God himself. God became, so to speak, a displaced person. There was nowhere for him to dwell; no spot where imagination could place his throne and the seat of his divine justice. Stubbornly, often stupidly, religion resisted the displacement of the God who was a greatly magnified person, a separate being apart from, above, and beyond the world. Yet slowly, inevitably, this idea of God has had to be abandoned.

In simplest terms, the idea of God as the "Man Upstairs" falls today because in this wild, vast universe, we cannot imagine where "upstairs" might be. The rediscovery of God in our day, at its deepest levels, begins with this negative realization that God cannot be a separate, powerful being who dwells "out there" or "upstairs" or anywhere else. The effect of this realization—which is largely the work of science—upon religion is summed up in these words of the contemporary theologian Paul Tillich:

> If you start with the question whether God does or does not exist, you can never reach him; and if you assert that he does exist, you can reach him even less than if you assert that he does not exist. A God about whose existence or non-existence you can argue is a thing beside others within the universe of existing things. And the question is quite justified whether such a thing does exist and the answer is equally justified that it does not exist. It is regrettable that scientists believe that they have refuted religion when they rightly have shown that there is no evidence whatsoever for the assumption that such

a being exists. Actually, they have not only not refuted religion, but they have done it a considerable service. They have forced it to reconsider and to restate the meaning of the tremendous word God.*

This rethinking of the meaning of the word God will lead us eventually into a whole new area of experience and understanding. God is to be sought and found, not in the starry heavens nor in the depths of the material earth, but within the human spirit itself. The seers and mystics of many ages and many different religions have always insisted that this was the case. God is not a being among other beings. He is the Ground of All Being. God is not a thinker and a knower. He is that foundation of thought and knowledge beneath us which makes thinking and knowing possible. God is not a person who knows us and loves us. He is that power within us and within all life by virtue of which it is possible for man to love. God is not the engineer of the universe running it like a machine. He is that universal creativity, order, and meaning of which we ourselves and all things are parts.

We seek and in some measure find the reality of God, not by argument and proof, and not by frantically seeking here and there, but by quiet, steady growth in self-understanding, by the stripping away of the outward and superficial thoughts and activities of life, by a process of self-realization which shows us ourselves as we truly are. God, the oriental monarch, the benevolent tyrant, the "Man Upstairs," is lost, and rediscovered as that ground of calmness, of meaning, of trust, and of love out of which our own courage, strength, and purposefulness grow. We do not demand of God, as Joshua and Moses did and many modern statesmen do, that he assist us in furthering our foreign policy, thwart and destroy our enemies, and bring us to victory and prosperity. Rather, in quietness and confidence, we seek that ground of meaning and love which shall enable us humbly to bring meaning and love into our own lives.

* Paul Tillich in *Man's Right to Knowledge,* Second series: *Present Knowledge and New Directions,* New York, Columbia University Press, 1955, p. 79.

It is a strange thing that at the very moment in history when East finds itself arrayed against West, when Asia stands in a posture of rejection and revolt against Europe and America, the best thought of the Judeo-Christian West should be groping towards some of the deepest spiritual insights of the East. For the high religions of the East, in particular Hinduism and Buddhism, have always regarded the idea of the "Man Upstairs" as a primitive and immature notion of the basic spiritual reality. They have sought to help men over the paths of contemplation and self-understanding into the attitudes of compassion and peace. They have been less creative outwardly, less aggressive in a social and political sense, but also more tolerant, more humble, and more charitable. They have learned from Christian civilization, perhaps only too well and too rapidly, that it is possible for men to transform the material world in their own interests. Perhaps we can learn from their great tradition of contemplation and spiritual depth that a materially transformed world can still be a hell on earth unless men can find and learn to live out of the spiritual depths within their own souls more deeply than we have done so far.

At any rate, the direction which the rediscovery of God in our time is taking leads towards a new emphasis on the contemplative side of life, a deliberate withdrawal from incessant activity for at least as long as it takes to find out what kind of activity is meaningful and what kind is merely futile busyness. It requires a steady and deliberate effort on the part of the individual to reawaken the power of independent thought as over against the conformist thinking which church, state, and society seem constantly to demand of him. It requires a quickening of genuine human feeling as against the stylized emotions of hate, fear, anger, and retaliation which patriotism and nationalism are constantly demanding that we feel. The rediscovery of God will require that each person fight a war of liberation for the control of his own mind and spirit against the tyranny of mass thinking and mass emotion. The rediscovery of God, as it proceeds, and it certainly has a long way to go, will result in more and more people who are deeply conscious of their own unique individuality and, therefore, deeply respectful towards the individuality of other persons.

The rediscovery of God will result in a slow lifting of the burden of anxiety from our shoulders, for it will mean that we no longer see ourselves, as we so often do today, as entrusted with the entire destiny of all creation. Rather, we will be aware of ourselves as part of a deeper, more real order and meaning within which our task is not to be responsible for everything. "What stands in your way," said the Zen teacher to his overzealous pupil, "is that you have a much too wilful will. You think that what you do not do yourself does not happen."

We have looked, and continue to look in these days, because it is our habit so to do, for a rediscovery of God which will sweep the nation with dramatic suddenness, winning hosts of the unconverted to vigorous, articulate, muscular faith. Yet, perhaps the more important rediscovery of God has been quietly going on all the time and will manifest itself in quite different ways:

> In a slow return to sanity, tolerance, humor and patience in our national and international affairs, as well as in our personal lives.
>
> In a more realistic acceptance of the world as it is and of ourselves as we are, and a gentle wisdom born of knowing that we cannot be and do everything.
>
> In a mellowing of the dogmatism which so often today makes us feel that he who sees life differently must be a threat to our own security.
>
> Above all, in a renewed capacity for enjoyment of the world and of one another, for laughter, for relaxation, for pity and compassion, and for peace.

"The chief end of man," says the Westminster catechism, "is to glorify God and enjoy him forever." We have all but forgotten what a statement like that could mean. God has been for so long in our thoughts the tyrant, the driver, the source of the uneasy conscience, the judge before whom we feel guilty and afraid. And when we could not bear this kind of God any longer, we threw him out entirely and found ourselves more lonely and lost than ever before, for the "Man Upstairs" behind "clouds of lace" is no real substitute. We were unwise to abandon the quest for God. He was as great as our minds could comprehend and our hearts imagine. But as our minds grow larger, and our hearts more open and compassionate, a greater and truer God appears. He is not above us and beyond us; he is within us and among us. He does not rule and drive us, but in the knowledge of him we learn to rule ourselves. He does not dwell in the heavens. Rather, he is our dwelling place in all generations. "In him we live and move and have our being."

Some of us deny even that God exists; some don't think the question is important. There are four different attitudes about the existence of God: atheism, agnosticism, humanism, theism.

Atheism is the positive conviction that there is no God. Atheism is an act of faith. The atheist concludes that nothing in the available evidence seems to indicate the existence of God and that everything tends to deny it. His affirmation is that there is no God.

The Agnostic holds the conviction that the ultimate question of the existence or non-existence of God is unanswerable in terms of the human mind. The agnostic neither affirms nor denies the existence of God. He simply says that we do not know and cannot know.

The humanist is something of an agnostic. He probably agrees that we do not know and cannot know of the existence of God, but he does not leave the matter there. Whatever notions of God man may have, the humanist says, are his own creation. "An honest God is the noblest work of man." The humanist is often content to leave the great speculative question of God's existence in abeyance. He is interested primarily in the growth and enrichment of the human spirit; in the fulfilment of the great human purposes of justice, truth, freedom, and love. He does not see that the theoretical question of God has any particular bearing on these efforts of man, and he can point to ample evidence that sometimes preoccupation with the idea of God has prevented men from getting on with the human enterprises that needed to be carried out.

The thoughtful theist today is probably also a humanist in a sense. He would agree with the humanist about the great human tasks of justice, freedom, truth, and love, and about the great goal of realizing the highest possible development of the human spirit. But in addition to this, he has a positive intuition that some power and purpose greater than man's is also involved in this process. He sees himself and all men as related to this inclusive and continuing power and purpose of God. Not only does he care about the great human purposes and values, he believes that somehow God cares about them, too, and lends strength and courage to men in their efforts to realize them.

Like the atheist, the theist examines the evidence available to him, and often it is much the same evidence, and makes his act of faith in the proposition that there is God. What is the real difference between the two? I suspect that in each case a man becomes a theist or an atheist not for theological reasons or on rational grounds but out of deep feelings and impulses, desires and experiences. The atheist has perhaps a profound desire for independence, having suffered much under arbitrary authority in home or church or school or state. He wants to feel with William Ernest Henley:

> I am the captain of my soul,
> I am the Master of my fate.

The theist, on the other hand, may have known a kindly and more reasonable authority in his life, one which did not drive and compel but guided and led, and released him into liberty and responsibility step by step. Far from feeling rebellious at this authority, he has learned to trust it and to find strength and vision in it. Hence it seems natural to him, as his vision of himself and the world grows to extend this kindly and creative authority until it encompasses his life and all life. Just as it is natural for the atheist to assert his independence, it is natural for the theist to examine his experience and feel the ring of truth in Wordsworth's poem "Lines Composed a Few Miles above Tintern Abbey."

> And I have felt
> A presence that disturbs me with the joy
> Of elevated thoughts; a sense sublime
> Of something far more deeply interfused,
> Whose dwelling is the light of setting suns,
> And the round ocean and the living air,
> And the blue sky, and in the mind of man:
> A motion and a spirit that impels
> All thinking things, all objects of all thought,
> And rolls through all things.

Likewise the agnostic and the humanist have much in common. Each is willing to be tentative about ultimate answers. The difference is that while the pure agnostic does not believe in the possibility of ultimate answers, the humanist finds them not in the great speculative questions but in those ethical goals and values which he declares to be central in the life of man.

Clarence Darrow, the great trial lawyer, once debated publicly with Dr. Shirley Jackson Case of the University of Chicago on the subject: "Has Christianity Failed?" Darrow, of course, took the affirmative. But Dr. Case won the argument when he said that Darrow himself was an argument against the failure of Christianity, for he lived as close to the Golden Rule of Jesus as anyone he had ever known.

God is not a thing out there, or a person like you or me, separate and distinct from all other persons. God is a principle of power and purpose which results in action. God is not a static Noun. He is more like a Verb. God is not a rigid concept to be established or disposed of by our reasoning and argument. God is something that happens, that changes men and, through them, the world. God is a certain vitality and creativeness at the foundations of the world and in the mind and activity of man. He is alive, not dead. He lives and moves and has his being and works through what men are and what they do. We shall never catch him in a formal concept, no matter how subtle and comprehensive it may be. God is like the river that continues to flow, endlessly, powerfully through the deeps and mysteries of man's spirit, nourishing him, challenging him, sustaining him, pushing him on.

With some of these intuitions in mind, I recently turned to the Bible again and re-read some of the stories and experiences which there set forth the activities of God. In the opening pages of Genesis, in the magnificent legends of the creation of the world and of man, God is active. He labors for six days to make earth and sea and sky, plants, animals, birds, and all things necessary for life. Then stooping down, he fashions man of the dust of the ground and breathes into his nostrils the breath of life, and man becomes a living soul. And, according to the legend, when it was done, God, like any man who has been working hard, sat back and rested for a day and looked with satisfaction upon his work and said to himself: "Behold, it is very good."

How shall we translate this myth into the terms of our own thought and feeling? Perhaps we can say: "God is that which creates, anywhere and everywhere in the midst of life: in nature, in science, in art, in human relations, in society." Wherever something fresh, original, beautiful, alive, emerges in the world around you, in nature and in yourself, there God has been present and has passed by.

God appears in the Bible again and again as the one who stirs up men to adventure and discovery. He incites Abraham to set out upon a pilgrimage in his old age, leaving behind his security, to find a land which shall be for his children's children to inherit and enjoy. He is that strange impulse and movement in the life of the Patriarch which tells him that he must get up and be on his way even though he is old, that his life is not yet over, but only beginning. God is in the restlessness and hunger of the human spirit which sends men out to seek and to find what is as yet unrealized and only dimly seen. God is that which arouses in man the sense of his own power and possibility, and enables him to attempt, and sometimes to achieve, what most people think impossible. Perhaps we may say that insofar as your soul is stirred and allured by adventure, it is nourished and sustained by the living God.

When the people of Israel went out of Egypt under the leadership of Moses, it is said that God went before them as a pillar of cloud by day and a pillar of fire by night. In their hunger, he fed them; in their controversies, he gave them the law, in their conflicts he fought beside them and through their leaders he led them into freedom and the promised land. How shall we translate these tales except to say that the people who wrote and lived the Bible had found within their own living experience some principles of liberty and order and courage which were not empty theories but vital commands which reached and touched their consciences and which resulted in action? Whatever in man's experience liberates him from bondage, helps him achieve higher law and more just order in his common life, gives him courage in time of opposition and guidance in time of confusion and bewilderment is a sign of the presence and activity of the living God.

The word of God is constantly referred to in the Bible. It is not a mere word. It seems to be conceived as something which lives and acts. "His word runneth very swiftly." It "goes forth from Zion." "It breaks out like fire among the people." It carries with it judgement of evil, condemnation, mercy, forgiveness, pity, hope, confidence. God is depicted in the Bible as leading man "beside the still waters," "restoring his soul, leading him in the paths of righteousness." Even though man walks through the valley of the shadow of death, he shall fear no evil, for God is with him. In one of the most dramatic of the Psalms, man is described as one who has run away from God and tried to hide from him only to cry out at last:

O Lord thou hast searched me and known me, Thou knowest my downsitting and mine uprising. Thou understandest my thought afar off. Thou compassest my path and my lying down and art acquainted with all my ways. Whither shall I go from thy spirit and whither shall I flee from thy presence. If I ascend up into heaven, behold thou art there. If I make my bed in hell, behold thou art there. If I take the wings of the morning and dwell in the uttermost parts of the sea, even there shall thy hand lead me and thy right hand shall hold me. If I say, surely the darkness shall cover me, even the night shall be light about me. Yea, the darkness hideth not from thee, but the light shineth as the day. The darkness and the light are both alike to Thee.

How shall we translate this except to say that God is the one who is always present, who cannot be escaped? He works in the judgement which convicts our consciences, in the tenderness that permits us to forgive others and ourselves, in the reassurance that comes in time of weariness, in the courage that comes in time of decision and accomplishment, in the reminder that comes in time of forgetfulness and alienation.

God appears among the prophets of Israel as the enemy of insincerity and empty show, the lover of integrity, honesty, justice, and compassion. He is not interested in sacrifices and rituals. He wants the poor to get a fair deal. He wants the stranger to be treated with kindness. He wants wars to cease and swords to be beaten into ploughshares. He wants kings to rule with equity and understanding. He wants the strong to stop oppressing the weak. And if these things are not done, this living, acting God warns, he will do a terrible thing. "I will bring upon this people the fruit of their own thoughts." That is to say, the injustice and cruelty they inflict upon others will inevitably turn back upon themselves.

How shall we translate this? Perhaps we may say that wherever in our land or across the world today men are struggling to help their brothers up towards better life, towards health and strength and knowledge and freedom, there the living God is at work. And if we say this, we must also say with all solemnity that wherever men are struggling to hold their brothers down, to perpetuate their misery and hunger, to set themselves up as superior to other men, to justify cruelty and maintain oppression, there the judgement of the living God of history will be felt: "I will bring upon this people the fruit of their own thoughts."

In the greatest pages of the Old Testament and in the New Testament, God is the Comforter, the Redeemer, the One who suffers with his people in their sufferings and promises that at last out of their failure and defeat shall come their victory and his. Jesus said: "I must be about my Father's business." It is not the phrase of a mystic or a philosopher. It is the notion of a most practical and busy God, who has a lot of things to do within and among his people and expects some help and cooperation from them. Jesus was apparently committed to the vision of the active God. "Not every one that says unto me, 'Lord, Lord,' shall enter into the kingdom of heaven, but he that does the will of my Father who is in heaven."

How shall we translate this except to say that the authentic godliness, the essential activity of the divine in the midst of life is seen and known and judged in the light of what we are and what we do? Wherever in the world people are actually trying with patience and courage to do the will of God, to express this vital inward reality which changes men and situations, which infuses love and justice into places which have been filled with hate and oppression, there the living God is present and active. The degree of our faith in God is measured not by our words or the cleverness and subtlety of our argument but by how much justice, how much love, how much pity, how much peace emanates from us into the world around us.

Therefore, if you do not have a nice, orderly concept of God, well founded in reason and philosophy, buttressed by learned arguments and theories, never mind. God is a vital expression in the midst of life of the values which matter most. Wherever that vital expression takes place, there is God, but you will not find him until you become part of the effort.

How can we expect to believe in freedom as a high value until we have thrown ourselves into the struggle to set men free? How can we care for brotherhood as an ideal until we have had some practice in seeing and facing and working through the problems which arise when we try in the midst of life, in our own relationships in our own community, to make brotherhood work? How can we believe in peace until we have wrestled with ourselves and others in order to achieve something of the wisdom, self-control, understanding, and compassion which make peace possible? And how can we believe in God until we have had some part in the effort to realize the values for which God lives and works in the world?

The God who will be reluctantly drafted to do his bit for the party or the nation is not really there at all. The living God, the God who creates, sends men out to adventure and discovery, judges, forgives, makes whole, hates injustice, loves mercy, honors truth, labors for peace and, in all the process, suffers and works with and for his people. He is not the big man upstairs. He is that profound mysterious vitality and sense of purpose which every man can feel in his own heart and know himself to be involved with. He is in the awakened, uneasy conscience. He is in the mounting impatience with all that is mediocre and second-rate. He is in the compassion that is stronger than hatred and the understanding that is deeper than enmity. He is in the human action which leads at length to profound belief and perhaps at last to comprehension. Life comes first, then faith, then understanding. We have had things the wrong way around for a long time. We have thought: first we must understand, then we can believe, and then we shall act for justice, for liberty, for brotherhood, for peace. And this process has too often been the excuse for inaction, the justification for indifference. Jesus said, "If any man will do His will, he shall know of the doctrine." He was right. He that shall do the work shall know God.

Seven The Meaning of Prayer

The popular spokesmen of the current revival of religion have much to say about the importance of prayer. From Dr. Peale and others you can procure "prayer cards" which will tell you how to go about praying for the resolution of certain problems such as business reverses, family complications, hostile feelings towards others, sickness, worry, and anxiety. In most of our major cities today, there are several phone numbers you can call at any time of the day or night, and you will hear a minister's voice, recorded on tape, utter a brief prayer or message of inspiration. You will find selected blessings on many restaurant tables along with the menu. President Eisenhower has, according to his minister, Dr. Elson of the National Presbyterian Church in Washington, "popularized prayer and righteousness." And Washington is now "a praying city."

All this may very well be good and constructive. I have no wish to criticize it. People come to the experience of religion over many ways, and no one of us is wise enough to say that a way which leads men to better, more serene and useful life is not a good and constructive way. Nor is there any doubt that an authentic reawakening of the religious spirit will involve a renewed emphasis upon the contemplative side of life, the rediscovery of old practices of prayer and meditation, or the creation of new ones better suited to the needs and experiences of men in this age. But I am sure that many people in this age are beyond the reach of the appeal to prayer now being so widely promoted. We know all too well and feel all too keenly the need for some sort of deep and personal communion with ourselves, with others, and with life's underlying meaning and purpose, but we are not able to accept this experience in the terms of man as the suppliant and God—all too much like a man made large—as the dispenser of favors and assistance in response to the suppliant's requests and prayers. In the 1920's James Branch Cabel, in one of his essays, raised the impudent question of why it should be necessary for him, who tried to be a rational human being, to enter a dark building adorned with a phallic symbol at 11 o'clock on a Sunday morning, and listen to a fellow dressed in a black nightgown direct impossible and pompous petitions in archaic language to somebody who obviously was not there. Bitter and cynical as the question is when stated in this way, I am sure that millions of thoughtful men and women who genuinely want to grow spiritually are perplexed by the facile forms of prayer now being offered on the popular market. They are willing to consider the idea of prayer, but it must be something more than mere petition addressed to somebody who obviously is not there.

Lewis Mumford, in his searching book, *The Conduct of Life*, discusses the need for leading "a double life." By this he means that if our experience is to be meaningful, if we are to learn from what happens to us, then we must develop the skill of reflecting regularly upon life as we live it. We must learn to live each experience over again in a mood of calmness and with the purpose of trying to see how it fits into the whole pattern of our living. We must take time to do this even to the point of deliberately withdrawing from activities which might be considered quite useful and necessary, to be sure that those we do continue to carry are carried thoughtfully rather than superficially, calmly rather than frantically. The most comprehensive definition of prayer is that it is a process of orderly reflection upon what we are, what we have done, what we propose to do, and what it all means in the larger framework of our highest values and our basic responsibilities as human beings. In this sense, there is hardly anyone who has not practiced prayer, however fitfully, and no one who does not feel the need for it.

It helps also to keep in mind that petition, the effort to get something which will be helpful to us or to solve a pressing problem, while it is a part of prayer, is only a small, perhaps even an incidental, part of the whole process. Prayer does include desire which is often expressed in the form of petition. Indeed one familiar definition of prayer is "the soul's sincere desire, expressed, or unexpressed." But in order to see the proper place of petition in the total activity of prayer, we must look at some of its other aspects.

The great traditional ways of Christian prayer have usually included five distinct parts: 1. Thanksgiving and Praise; 2. Self-examination and Confession; 3. Meditation; 4. Petition and Intercession; 5. Contemplation. Each one of these parts is important to all the others. Each represents an attitude of mind and spirit essential to a sound religious life. Taken together, they add up to the "double life"—the life of profound and thoughtful reflection upon our experience of which Mr. Mumford writes so persuasively. At the start, we should empty our minds of the idea that prayer depends upon the use of particular words and phrases drawn from the archaic language of the past. It does not matter whether you think of God as "Thou" or "You." It does not matter that your prayer should imitate the stately language of the King James Bible or the Book of Common Prayer. Nor do attitudes of body such as kneeling, closing the eyes or bowing the head have any significance except as they aid in concentration of the mind. There was an old gentleman who used to attend a church where I was once minister. Throughout the prayer he would sit with his head held high and his eyes wide open. Once he explained the reason for this to me. "I have always felt," he said, "that when I come into the presence of my Creator he will want me to hold my head high and look him straight in the eye and answer for what I am and what I have done." Perhaps the gentleman lacked humility, but I loved him for his honesty and integrity, and I suspect his Creator, to whom he has long since gone, may also have loved him for the same reasons. Prayer is essentially a mental and an emotional discipline, a training of the mind and will. It does not depend upon words and gestures but upon the honesty and integrity and the patience with which we undertake to live the double life of action and orderly reflection upon the meaning of our action.

The first of the five component parts of prayer is thanksgiving. Everyone has experienced it, not only in the form of gratitude towards specific persons for specific gifts and benefits but in that more general gratitude which moves a man simply to appreciate and enjoy the world and the wonder of life, and the variety of possibilities and challenges which fill it. Many of the great traditional ways of prayer open on the note of praise and thankfulness. Sometimes that thankfulness is directed to God as the Giver of every good and perfect gift. "O give thanks unto the Lord, for he is good; for his mercy endureth forever." Sometimes that thankfulness is simply man's spontaneous rejoicing in the fact of his own life, in the lives of others, in the world of nature, in the wonder and beauty of being alive. The note of authentic prayer is in Edna St. Vincent Millay's familiar sonnet:

> O world, I cannot hold thee close enough.
> Thy winds, thy wide gray skies.
> Thy mists that roll and rise.
> Thy woods, this autumn day, that ache and sag
> And all but cry with color. That gaunt crag
> To crush. To lift the lean of that black bluff.
> World, world, I cannot get thee close enough.
> Long have I known a glory in it all,
> But never knew I this;
> Here such a passion is
> As stretcheth me apart. Lord, I do fear
> Thou'st made the world too beautiful this year.
> My soul is all but out of me—let fall
> No burning leaf; prithee, let no bird call.*

But you do not have to be a poet, for these things are often expressed in quite ordinary ideas and feelings: "It

* From *Collected Poems,* Harper & Brothers, copyright © 1913, 1941 by Edna St. Vincent Millay.

is a beautiful day, and the sky is clear and blue. The air is like wine, and there is a spring in my step and joy in my work. All the people I work with seem beautiful to me, and I am glad to be alive." What we so often forget is that this, too, is prayer, as authentic and profound as the feelings of any poet or saint. Everyone partakes of this experience at least occasionally. When he does so he should remember that this is prayer.

Everyone also knows something of self-examination and confession. The confessional as a formal institution of religion no longer exists except within the Catholic and Anglican churches. But it is practiced in many ways in our society. It is necessary for man to examine his life, to make searching and thoughtful judgements, to measure his words and acts by the standards of necessity and excellence. Often he needs help in this process from the outside. The minister, the doctor, the lawyer, the counselor, the teacher, the friend, all in their various ways help people to perform the function of the confessional. They listen with understanding and sympathy. They attempt to help clarify the situation rather than to judge it. They enable people to be honest with themselves. The prayer of self-examination and confession goes on constantly within our minds and hearts. It is a necessity of self-knowledge and self-understanding. Socrates said that the "unexamined life is not worth living." We must examine ourselves to find out who we really are, what we mean, what we most truly want to be. And in this process we must strip away the many self-deceptions and evasions which we all practice. Eckhart, the fourteenth-century mystic, wrote of this process:

> A man has many skins in himself, covering the depths of his own heart. Man knows so many things. He does not know himself. Why thirty or forty skins or hides, just like an ox's or a bear's, so thick and hard, cover the soul. Go into your own ground and learn to know yourself there.*

* Raymond B. Blakney, *Meister Eckhart: A Modern Translation*, Harper & Brothers, New York, 1941.

In self-examination, we try to get outside ourselves so that we can see ourselves as we truly are. We put aside the flattery or the condemnation which the world accords to that part of us which the world can see. We disengage ourselves from the illusions and poses which make up so large a part of our active daily life. We try to dig deep beneath the impressions which we make on others, the picture of ourselves which we would like the world to see, and find out what we are really worth. If we are faithful and patient, a new picture of ourselves begins to emerge. It may not be as handsome a picture, but it is probably more honest. We accept our limitations. We admit that we are not as good as we would wish people to think we are, nor indeed as good as in our hearts we truly want to be. We feel shame and remorse but with them a kind of self-acceptance. Perhaps we feel something of what Noah said when he met "De Lawd" in Marc Connelly's *The Green Pastures:* "I ain't very much but I'se all I got."

If your religious faith includes belief in God, then your self-examination may well be expressed in the spirit of the 139th Psalm: "O Lord, thou hast searched me and known me. Thou knowest my downsitting and mine uprising. Thou understandest my thought afar off. For there is not a word in my mouth but lo, O Lord, thou knowest it altogether." Or it may find expression in the words of the General Confession: "We have erred and strayed from thy ways like lost sheep. We have followed too much the devices and desires of our own hearts. We have offended against thy holy laws. We have left undone those things which we ought to have done and we have done those things which we ought not to have done . . ." But if you cannot believe in a God who knows you through and through, if this concept of deity simply does not make sense to your mind, you can still go into the quiet of your own soul, search your own heart and mind in an effort to win inner honesty, integrity and self-knowledge. And this also is prayer.

Honest self-examination leads on to meditation: the effort to think things through imaginatively and sensitively until we know what we ought to do and be, or at least until we can see what the next step is. A good deal of what is loosely called meditation today is not much more than idle day-dreaming and woolgathering. Meditation is directed thought, a sober effort to clarify the main purposes and meanings of our life. It is hard intellectual work and requires a high degree of concentration and persistence. It is the attempt to increase wisdom through imagination.

Some years ago, on a college campus, I was present with a group of other men when a wise, old Catholic priest conducted a meditation on the parable of the Good Samaritan. You would think that everything which can be said about this familiar parable has been said a thousand times over. But not so. He made us see the story for the first time. More than that, he made us live it. It was an exercise in role-playing. We played the role first of the man who fell among thieves, was beaten, robbed, and left for dead beside the road. We thought of his pain and surprise, of his plans which were disrupted, his terrible need, his pathetic disappointment as priest and Levite approached and then passed him by on the other side of the road. We played the parts of priest and Levite. What were their errands? Doubtless to them they seemed so pressing that they could not stop to help the wounded man. Why did they pass by on the other side? Was it cruelty or ignorance? Was it indifference or a willful blindness to what was most important? We asked ourselves whether we too had done as much. We played the part of the Samaritan. Was he also busy and rushed? What was the difference in him that made him forget his preoccupations and stop and help the victim beside the road? We pondered the fact that the Jews had no dealings with Samaritans and scorned them as an inferior race. Yet here was this Samaritan doing his utmost to help a member of a race which hated and scorned him. At length there was a pause which lasted several minutes and then the old priest said quietly: "Which one of these people are you now? Which one of them do you most truly want to be?"

The questions were like an electric shock. We realized that in our various ways we had played all these roles in life: victim, priest, Levite, Samaritan, even the thieves. We also knew which one of the characters in the story we ought to be and wanted to be. We knew our need and desire, and so the meditation led quite naturally into the prayer of petition.

Petition begins when we know what at our best we ought to be and want to be. It is the effort to leap the chasm between intention and act, between thought and deed. Only if we come to petition without the previous disciplines of self-examination and meditation will we fall into the trap of presenting cheap and trivial desires as part of our prayer. If our self-examination has been rigorously honest and our meditation thoughtful and deep, these mediocre desires will have been sifted out of us. Petition has been a badly abused form of prayer, mainly because of that narrowness of understanding which leads most people to see prayer as petition only. But if we can think of petition not as an effort to persuade "somebody up there" to give us what we want but rather as the effort to bring our desires refined by careful thought and understanding, into the presence of the highest we know, then perhaps petition may be more understandable.

Primitive man saw the whole world as alive with divinity. He prayed to trees and stones and rivers and mountains, and to the sun, moon, and stars. He offered his petitions spontaneously for everything that affected his life. For him there was no realization of a natural order of things which operated according to certain laws. If it rained, the gods desired it so. If there was an earthquake or a storm the gods were angry. If the crops were good, the gods were in a benevolent mood. If someone was sick, he had a demon. If he got well, the demon had been driven out.

For primitive man, prayer was the method by which one got on the good side of the gods and persuaded them to do the things which were helpful rather than harmful to man. Modern man supposes that he has left all this far behind, but in reality much of his prayer is of the same primitive sort. He prays that his nation may be blessed and its enemies destroyed. He prays for success, prosperity, peace of mind, and a resolution of all his problems. He hopes for the miracle which will relieve him of the consequences of his own foolish thoughts and acts. He, too, tries to get on the good side of God. Yet we should not blame him too much unless his prayer begins and ends with these primitive and natural desires. If, beginning here, he goes on until he learns to think of the prayer of petition not as the effort to get the "Man Upstairs" to side with him but as his own effort to express his desires in a creative and meaningful pattern, he is growing towards a deeper understanding of prayer. His desires will be judged, many of them rejected, and the best of them at last expressed in prayer which is the "soul's sincere desire." If God is love, we dare not bring before him desires which are contrary to love. If God is truth we dare not offer him desires which arise from our dishonesty and self-deception. If God is the God of all men we dare not present to him desires which would result in our being singled out for special privilege. If God is beauty, we dare not offer him the meanness and ugliness in our own souls. Thus disciplined petition does refine our desires until those which we presume to present in prayer are the best we have. Even those desires must be offered in the full realization that in the light of a wisdom greater than ours and a love more perfect than any we know, they may not be possible or even good. It is probably fortunate that some of the desires for which we prayed most earnestly were never realized. They might well have resulted in our destruction. The best prayer always contains something of the spirit which Jesus expressed when he prayed that he might be spared the ordeal of disgrace and crucifixion: "Father, if it be possible, let . . . this pass from me. Nevertheless, not my will but thine be done." In the simple, direct expression of our best desires for ourselves, for others, and for the world we are not challenging God to interrupt his order and break his own laws on our behalf. Rather we are seeking to understand that order more truly and find our own place and responsibility within it. Lincoln said of his own prayers that he was not trying to find out whether God was on his side, but whether he was on God's side.

One phase of the prayer of petition is called intercession, prayer for others. Those whom we love, those for whom we are deeply concerned, our friends, our country, the causes which seem most important to us, even our enemies quite naturally are ever present in our minds. They all have their places in our desires and thoughts. It is only natural that we should carry these concerns with us in our prayer. It is said of the Swiss pastor Jean Friedrich Oberlin that on Saturday mornings he went alone into his church and sat successively in the pews usually occupied by those whom he knew to be in special need. As he sat there he pondered those needs, held each person, as it were, in the presence of God, and tried to figure out what he, Oberlin, could do to help. Whatever your views may be about the theology of prayer, this kind of sensitive human concern is a positive value in the world which gives expression to neighbor-love and helps increase its power. We are a long way from understanding the mysterious processes whereby minds work upon one another in this life, and it may be that your charitable thoughts, your profound loyalties, your longing that another person may realize the best that is in him have more real results than you can imagine or explain. Furthermore prayer for others is incipient action. You cannot hold other people prayerfully in your mind for very long without being led, even driven, to try to do something to help them. The prayer of intercession is an affirmation of that deep human concern, that sense of mutual dependence and fellowship which holds the world together. However we may formulate or explain such prayer, it has tangible effects. Your prayer that your friend may recover from illness may not cure the illness, but it may lead you to bring him comfort and help of inestimable value, and that comfort and help may contribute to his cure. In this sense, every thoughtful word, every kind act is a prayer of intercession.

Beyond these more active forms of prayer in which we express our feelings, thoughts, desires, and concerns, there is an area which can be called contemplation. Here the mind and feelings become still. We do nothing, think nothing, say nothing, seek nothing but are simply open and receptive. This is perhaps the most difficult thing that modern man can be asked to do, for it is his habit to be always on the move, always busy, always active. Silence is abhorrent to him. Solitude is a condition to be avoided at any cost. Inactivity seems a sin. Yet all of us need from time to time to step aside from the world and its concerns, to "be still and know," to receive rather than to give, to be inwardly renewed and restored. There are depths in the human spirit beneath all words, ideas, and activities. In that part of prayer which is called contemplation, a man quietly and reverently lets go of the world around him with all its pressures and concerns and goes down into those depths. The contemplative silence is a familiar thing to all kinds of people: to scientists, poets, artists, men of affairs, as well as to thinkers, prophets, and saints. Out of it have come some of their most creative insights, the necessary strength for the task to be done, the capacity to love and to serve and to care deeply. Many busy people have learned to make little islands of quiet contemplation in the midst of their day so that there will be time for them to collect themselves and bring to their most important decisions the perspective of a deep and quiet mind. I have found it helpful always to set aside for each appointment a little more time than is really needed so that there will be a few moments of peace and quiet between each set of problems and decisions.

John Masefield in his poem "The Everlasting Mercy" suggests the nature of contemplation in the words of his character Saul Cain:

> I did not think; I did not strive,
> The deep peace burnt me alive.

In contemplation man loses awareness not only of the world and its pressures but of the self and its insistent anxieties and demands. He is an empty vessel waiting to be filled with the living waters of truth and peace. The 23rd Psalm also suggests it: "He maketh me to lie down in green pastures. He leadeth me beside the still waters. He restoreth my soul."

Contemplation is as important to the atheistic Buddhist or to the polytheistic Hindu as it is to the monotheistic Jew or Christian or Moslem. There has always been a deep stream of contemplation which unites the great religions of mankind. The Hindu Gandhi, though he could not accept the claims of Christian theology, could feel quite at home with the long tradition of Christian prayer and contemplation, for except in outward terms it hardly differed from his own. And many a Christian has found his own inner life enriched and strengthened by contact with the Buddhist and Hindu ways of contemplation.

Contrary to popular opinion, prayer is not a magical formula which a person repeats when he cannot think of anything else to do. Prayer is hard intellectual labor, not the abandonment of thought and its disciplines but the effort to apply thought rigorously to the conditions of one's own life. Prayer is a training of the will, a conscious effort to control and direct one's feelings and affections towards that which is highest and best. Reasonableness, teachableness, openness of mind are constant necessities in prayer. Only when these disciplines have been accepted and used faithfully do men find in prayer the intuitions of spiritual reality, the replenishing of courage and strength, the deepening of love and compassion, the peace of mind which are so often claimed as the results of prayer. We are a long way here from prayer cards, little inspirational messages, and the superficial and superstitious repetition of comforting thoughts. Popular religion has transformed the noble, exacting and long path of prayer into a deceptively easy little walk. You do people no real service when you tell them that what is hard is easy and what is complex is simple.

But we must still face the questions raised by the cynical writer. To what or whom are we addressing all this? Does anybody listen to our thoughts or words when we pray? Does anybody care? Here it is necessary to distinguish between the God who is a person, just as you and I are persons, and the idea of a God who is apprehended as all-pervading reality, as a profound continuing spiritual force for truth and goodness and love. We cannot know such a God as a person. But we can perhaps feel in some sense personally related to such a God through the human responses of loyalty and concern and love. Prayer at its deepest and best is a sense of relationship, a feeling of being personally connected with and responsible to some power greater than the self. It is the sense of being part of that power, almost included within it, and of helping to carry out its tasks on earth. Its true nature is suggested in the words of St. Teresa of Avila:

> Christ has no body on earth now but yours, no hands but yours, no feet but yours. Yours are the eyes through which to look out Christ's compassion to the world. Yours are the feet with which he is to go about doing good, and yours are the hands with which he is to bless us now.

Only when we have abandoned the idea of prayer as a prop and a crutch to help us over the hard spots, and dared to face it as a means whereby we may offer ourselves to be used in the service of all that is best do we find its rewards of comfort and courage and increased power.

In our thinking about prayer, it is best to use the images and figures of speech which convey the notion of life and motion, of power and activity, rather than those which depict God as an oriental potentate seated on a throne and hearing and disposing of the requests of his servants. And here is one of our greatest difficulties. The traditional language of prayer does present the object of prayer either as a Lord and King or as a Father. Both figures have their significance but neither is adequate or accurate. It is here that "words strain, crack and sometimes break under the burden" of meaning they are required to carry. We must use some words in order to speak of that profound and powerful vitality with which prayer seeks to connect us. Yet any figures of speech we find are merely human and limited. They cannot carry the burden of the experience which is involved. Once we have grasped this we can approach the traditional words in a fresh way. We know that they are inadequate and inaccurate symbols. But we also know that through the centuries they have carried the real emotions, desires, thoughts and purposes of countless human beings as they tasted the deepest experiences of life. If we can keep in mind what the words stand for, the words will get in our way much less, and we may in time find better words for the fresh interpretation of that continuing experience.

There are two basic affirmations beneath the whole process of prayer, no matter how it may be expressed, no matter what structure of beliefs may surround it. Prayer affirms our awareness of the possibilities for growth and clarification within our own minds and hearts. It is possible to know ourselves better, to become wiser, more sensitive, more compassionate persons. Prayer also affirms that in and through this process, if one is faithful, if one is patient, one comes at last to feel a living sense of relationship, of cooperation, of trust and devotion to the source of all life and thought, to the foundations of meaning in one's own life and in the world.

We pray, not because we know God, but because we do not know him very well and long to know him better. We pray, not that we may have our desires fulfilled, but because we know that our desires must be judged and purified and tested. We pray not that we may receive the love of God but that we may be part of that love at work in the world. We pray because ever and again we are reminded of our connection with a power and purpose in life which we did not create and cannot control but through which our own small lives are dignified and made useful.

We pray in our several ways: some primitively, some superstitiously, some selfishly, some angrily; and some wisely, some humbly, some intelligently and lovingly. We pray because we are human, and ours is a vast, mysterious world with untold depths and possibilities.

We pray at first tentatively and haltingly. We hope for meanings. We search for the way. If we are faithful, if we are patient, if we persist, we come at length to a place of quietness and confidence where we find both perspective upon our lives as a whole and resources of courage and vision upon which we can draw in time of need. We learn the truth of the great biblical words: "They that wait upon the Lord shall renew their strength. They shall mount up with wings as eagles. They shall run and not be weary. They shall walk and not faint."

Eight Prayer and Work

There was in the fifth century a very holy man who became known as St. Simeon Stylites. He achieved this title for the remarkable feat of spending thirty-six years in constant prayer on top of a stone pillar in the Syrian desert. He was not unusual in his day and generation. It was a time when the dissolution of the Roman Empire —the greatest and most stable civilization which the world had known up to that time—had induced many thoughtful people to retire from the world, to renounce its joys and possibilities entirely, and to turn their attention wholly towards the contemplation of God and of the world to come. Out of this impulse grew at length the great Christian monastic orders—groups of men, and eventually of women, who had taken it upon themselves to give up the world as most of us know it, and turn their attention entirely to the living of the religious life in a community set apart from the world.

Whatever you may think of the motivations which lead men and women to make choices like this, and of the effects of those choices, it must be recalled that the monastic movements have made enormous contributions to our civilization. Had it not been for the religious orders of the so-called Dark Ages, much of the learning of the ancient world might have been lost to the modern world. Patiently, the monks copied ancient books and manuscripts, preserving them for future generations in a world which cared nothing for them. The religious communities became centers of learning and scholarship. Often too, they were the only groups interested in charity for the poor, care for the sick, comfort for the sorrowing and the bewildered. They were places where the disillusioned could find asylum and peace by giving themselves to a rule of life which set them apart as especially dedicated to the religious life in an irreligious world.

These impulses are still alive in our time, and thousands of men and women, mostly Catholic, have met the problem of life's anxiety and tension, and its apparent meaninglessness, by dedicating themselves to the religious life and giving themselves unselfishly to charitable, educational, or social service work with which the religious orders are concerned. Some few orders exist which are devoted entirely to prayer and carry on a ceaseless intercession for the world and the salvation of men.

Few of us are capable of the self-denial and renunciation required by such a life. Even if, at times, such a life seems desirable and a way out of a world of many perplexities and anxieties, most of us must live in the world as it is, work at its common tasks, fall in love, marry, raise children, try to make ends meet, and in the midst of all this do what we can to find resources of strength and courage which will be adequate to what is required of us. We must live in the world and find an effective balance between the external demands of work and all our other responsibilities and the internal necessities of prayer and a creative ordering of our lives. One of the central problems for modern man in his effort to achieve sanity and wholeness is the discovery of this creative relationship between work, in which word I include all the demands, personal, professional, social, and political which the outer world makes upon us, and prayer, by which I mean the entire inner activity of reflection and contemplation whereby meaning and direction are given to our work.

A common misunderstanding of prayer and of the whole contemplative aspect of life is to be found in the widespread impression that prayer and work, contemplation and action, are separate from and opposite to one another. Prayer is man's quest for deeper understanding of the highest values in his life and for the inner strength and vision which will help him to become what he most deeply wants to be when his thinking is clear and unclouded and his intention as pure as he can make it. Work is the effort to bring this intention about in the world as it actually is, with the circumstances as they are and within the limitations and incompleteness of our human nature. A sculptor looks at a piece of stone, and there exists in his mind some idea of the way in which he wishes to fashion this stone so that it will become a thing of meaning and beauty. That is his prayer. Then he takes hammer and chisel in hand and begins laboriously to chip away, attempting to transfer the idea from his mind to the stone. That is his work. If there were no idea and intention to begin with, the work of his hands would be nothing but busy work, mere activity. His labor would be empty and meaningless. If he never attempted to transfer the idea and intention from his mind to the stone, his prayer and desire, beautiful as they might be, would be useless. In all life, work without contemplation is blind. Contemplation without work is dead. Katherine Mansfield writes in her diary that she found that she could not pray at a certain period in her life because she had not been doing any work. For others, at certain times, the reverse would be equally true. They find that they cannot work well because they have not prayed, because, that is, they have lost or neglected the inward sense of worth and deep intention which gives meaning to the things they have to do. Prayer and work belong together. Each is important to the other. Each suffers if the other is lacking. If the work which once gave you joy and a sense of meaning in your life has now become dull and empty, it may be that the answer lies in a deepening of the contemplative side of your life. If you find contemplation and prayer futile and even unreal, it may be that you should re-examine the quality of your work and the reasons for which it is done.

The sound, religious life requires a sane and constructive balance between prayer and work and a sense of living connection between the two. There are two familiar symptoms which indicate that for a large number of persons in our time something has gone wrong with this balance. One is the very common observation that while the professed ideals of churches and religious people generally are very high and, probably for the most part, sincere, our work and activity not only fail to approach these ideals but sometimes seem to deny them outright. The unreligious are accustomed to say that the trouble with religious people is that they are one thing on Sundays and something quite different and opposite every other day of the week. There is enough truth in this criticism to demand that people who are concerned for religion take it seriously. Our work does fall short of our intentions and ideals, and sometimes what we do does deny what we pray for and profess to be. Some of this failure to practice what we preach is doubtless inherent in the human situation itself. But no honest religious person would want to deny the fact that he is not, in practice, as religious as he ought to be, and could be, and that this failure is sometimes due not alone to his natural human limitations but also to such attitudes as laziness, timidity, and lack of fidelity to his best ideals. In too many ways, our prayers and our ideals do not carry over into our work and practice, and this is true not only in the business world but in our home life and social life, in academic and professional life, and even in church life. Our spirituality suffers because the quality of our performance is mediocre.

The second symptom is of the opposite type. The balance between prayer and work is often destroyed by an overemphasis on mere activity. Work in itself can be a kind of sedative, and more often than we realize, the poverty of our contemplation drives us into a program of merely keeping busy so that we do not have to think and take stock of ourselves and where we are going. The merry-go-round is fun. It gives one the illusion of moving rapidly and purposefully. But you get off it at the same place where you got on. Few of us escape the haunting feeling that for all our activity and busyness we are not really going anywhere but simply moving round and round. We experience what Thomas Kelley called: "The poverty of our lives brought about by the overabundance of our opportunities." We work hard enough, but our work, robbed of its contemplation, becomes little more than occupational therapy, something to fill the emptiness of mind and spirit.

It is impossible to say which people are more unhappy and dangerous to themselves and others: those who pray without working at their prayers or those who work without prayer, merely to keep busy. The first group includes the hosts of the self-righteous and complacent who are ready to call anything good provided it makes no specific demands on them. The second group includes the hosts of the frustrated and the bored whose empty minds are like cups, aching to be filled with any kind of meaning, no matter how foolish or sinister, provided only they can keep busy.

A sane and saving religious faith is one which enables each one of us to find the proper balance and relationship between these two essential elements of prayer and work so that our contemplation has specific consequences in what we do and our work is dignified and directed by our contemplation.

Temperament has a good deal to do with the solutions to this problem which we find. For some kinds of people, the solution seems natural and reasonably easy. Prayer and work are so close together and interpenetrate each other so completely that they are honestly not aware of any separateness between the two. The authentic contemplative temperament, which is sometimes found in the artist, the poet, the saint, the philosopher, and occasionally in the teacher and the scholar, is often able to bring prayer and work so close that they seem to be identical.

Their work is primarily that of communicating what they know and have felt to be true to other people, and thus their work can flow naturally out of their thought and prayer. The meditative and reflective side of their nature is open at all times, and out of it comes their work.

Sometimes people of quite opposite temperament find the solution very simple. In a wonderful chapter, the writer of the book of Ecclesiasticus speaks of the important part which the ordinary craftsman and laborer plays in the life of a community. Such people, he says, are not heard in the public councils, nor do they sit high in the congregation, and they are not found where parables are spoken. Yet without them no city can be inhabited. "They will maintain the fabric of the world, and in the handiwork of their craft is all their prayer." To people of this temperament prayer and work are very nearly identical. Untroubled by perplexing doubts and questions, they do what they have skill to do as faithfully as they can. The record of one such soul has been preserved in a marvelous little book from the Seventeenth century called *The Practise of the Presence of God.* Nicholas Herman, who later became Brother Lawrence in a Carmelite monastery in Paris, was a man of no special skill or learning. He simply decided that he would do everything he did for the love of God. Entering the monastery he was quite content to do the lowliest and dirtiest tasks. Uncomplicated by any feelings of guilt or by any ambitions for knowledge and power, he quietly performed his simple tasks and discovered that in the midst of them he was able to live in the continuing presence of the Divine. If he did well, he thanked God that he had done so. If he did badly, he said innocently that "I shall never do any better unless You help me." He found the will of God in all things and declared that it was all the same to him whether he was washing pans in the monastery kitchen or kneeling before the altar at the Mass. God was equally present at all times and in all places. Prayer and work were identical.

Yet neither the pattern of the predominantly contemplative temperament sometimes found in saint, poet, and philosopher, nor that of the predominantly active and practical temperament as seen in Brother Lawrence will do for most of us. With full respect for Brother Lawrence, we can only conclude that he must have been, perhaps fortunately, quite untroubled by the deep doubts and speculative questions about the meaning of life which continually agitate most of us. He is not to be blamed for this. Perhaps he is to be envied. But his pattern is not ours.

If prayer and work cannot become identical—and for most of us they cannot—the next best thing is to keep alive the connection between them. This means that we will frankly recognize a real gap between the two which cannot be closed, but across which some kind of bridge can be thrown. We will see the religious problem as a question of alternation between prayer and work, a maintenance of some sort of communication system so that the quality and direction of our work is constantly judged and disciplined in prayer, and the sincerity of our prayer is constantly proved in work. This alternation is as simple and necessary as the alternation between sleeping, when we rest and are restored, and waking, when we expend the energy gathered in sleep. Or it is like eating, when we take into our bodies the food which gives us strength, and the activity which pours out that strength in work. When we are out of balance on either side of this equation, health and usefulness are diminished.

Because few of us at any time, and none of us at all times, are blessed with a constant sense of the Divine Presence, the gap between our prayer and our work must be bridged by recollection. Prayer is essentially a process which takes place when, in tranquility, we recollect our work and the experiences connected with it, try to see what it means, judge the quality of what we have been doing, and clarify our intentions and resolves as to what we shall do. Then we return to work with new perspective and new courage.

I do not know whether or not this observation has ever been studied clinically, but it appears to me that each life has its own special and individual rhythm and pace in this process of alternation between prayer and work. The rhythm and pace which is suitable to you may not be the one for me or for anyone else. Each must find his own. It is safe to say, however, that probably most of us require a certain period of quietness and opportunity for recollection each day. Such periods are very hard to find, not only in terms of time but in terms of place. The person who has found some way in which he can be both quiet and alone, for even a few minutes in a day, has achieved something rather rare in our modern culture. The person who has found such a time and place and has begun to use them for purposes of recollection and reflection on his work has begun the process of prayer.

Sometimes the rhythm of our lives seems to stretch over periods of time far longer than a single day or week. Looking back over the years, it is possible to see periods of several years when activity was at its height, followed by some months or years when activity died off, and there was a contemplative rhythm. A burst of activity is often followed by a time of quietness when the mind and spirit rest and receive instead of giving out, when they lie fallow, like a field, regaining their strength and richness for the next period of activity. Such times may seem outwardly to be times of uselessness or even laziness. Yet the soil must be restored before it can be productive again. Some day, I am sure, we shall know much more about this process of alternation than we do now and, knowing more about it, we shall know how to take advantage of it in terms of sane and healthy living. We should be spared a good deal of pain, anxiety, and guilt if we could learn to trust this process within our own lives. We should know, for example, that there are times when we are like the newly plowed field, ready to receive and nourish the seeds of new productiveness, ready for experiment and adventure, new ideas and new responsibilities. There are times when our lives should expand their horizons, when profound, long-contemplated changes should be made. And just as truly there are other times when we should—in the Quaker phrase—"center down," cut away everything that is not essential, simplify our hopes and desires, add nothing new but enter more deeply into what we have already begun. There are times when the best thing to do is nothing at all—a terrible thought to the contemporary mind, which seems to feel that it is always better to do something, even the wrong thing.

Slowly, if we can learn to examine our own lives deeply and honestly, we may come to perceive this principle of alternation as it operates in ourselves, the swinging of the pendulum between the need for work and the need for prayer and contemplation. Then we shall know that when our work becomes more and more hasty, feverish, anxious, and strained, what is needed is not anxiety and overconscientiousness but a pause, an act of recollection and re-appraisal of what we are and where we are going. And by the same token we shall know when the pause should end and the work begin again.

It is the beginning of a practical religious faith to discover and learn to trust this alternating rhythm in our own lives. It is the beginning of faith to know that if the work you have loved and enjoyed becomes dull and hateful the fault may be with oneself and not with the work and its meaning. The remedy may be not a frantic effort to keep up with one's responsibilities—always so far ahead of one's performance—but rather recollection and refreshment, and a new start, and a quiet confidence that both competence and enthusiasm will return. In the same way, if the faith which once inspired and encouraged you becomes doubtful and remote from your heart, the fault may be with your work and not with the foundations of your faith. Our ideal values have more reality and power when we are working actively to support and strengthen them. There is a direct relationship between your faith in any spiritual value and the intensity and fidelity of your work in helping to realize that spiritual value in the midst of your life and your community.

Brother Lawrence in his simplicity and innocence declared that for him the time of work differed not at all from the time of prayer. It was all the same. Meister Eckhart from the heights of his knowledge and speculative insight said much the same thing: "It is all one: what we plant in the soil of contemplation we shall reap in the

harvest of action . . . It is all a single process . . ." *
For most of us ordinary people, it is never quite as simple as that. We must move back and forth between the two worlds of prayer and work, giving each its due and permitting each to enrich and discipline the other. To us they seem different, these two worlds. In one we become familiar with hopes and dreams, ideal goals and purposes. In the other, we try to work out the intricate details whereby something of the ideal gets expressed in the ordinary course of life. Often while preoccupied with one we forget the other. It is no doubt, too bad, but that is the way it goes.

Since this is the situation, the task of religion becomes that of maintaining the connection between prayer and work, turning our attention now towards one, now towards the other, helping us, however slowly, to achieve that balance of faith and practicality, of inspiration and skill which shall make us both devout and practical in the service of all that is best.

One aspect of the present reawakening of interest in religion, which has received little attention but which may in the long run be of highest importance, is the appearance of a number of small groups which have focused their attention on the effort to restore the creative balance between prayer and work. Because the besetting sin of modern man is preoccupation with triviality, an inability to get outside the daily routine and see what it means and where it points, these groups have concentrated on the retreat technique. They have sought to provide busy and concerned people with an opportunity to withdraw from the immediate demands of their lives long enough for them to evaluate what they are doing and to be refreshed in company with others by silence, by manual labor, by solitary and group meditation and common worship under the leadership of a trained director. The purpose of these retreats, which usually last over a weekend from Friday evening until Sunday evening, is to provide

* Raymond B. Blakney, *Meister Eckhart: A Modern Translation*, Harper and Brothers, New York, 1941.

an opportunity for the "creative pause," so that busy people may withdraw from their immediate activities for a brief time, be refreshed in mind and spirit, and return to their tasks with a new perspective of what they mean. Readers who are interested in opportunities like this should consult an excellent little book by Professor Douglas V. Steere of Haverford College, *Time to Spare.**

The increase in the number of persons who learn to accept and practice the "creative pause" on a more or less regular basis will be an authentic sign that the renewed interest in religion in America is at work not only on superficial but profound and permanent levels. The seeds of the future in times of great historical crisis are apt to be found not in the popular mass movements of the day but in small groups of men and women who are seriously concerned about finding a new approach to the anxieties and uncertainties which beset them—not that they may have comfort and peace of mind, but that they may be more aware of what matters most, and better able to serve it in the world through their various occupations.

Emerson wrote that "Things are in the saddle and ride mankind." The effort to find a right balance between prayer and work is not a quest for freedom from the demands of "things," but a search for the ways in which we can win control over "things," center down to the significant and the essential, and find renewed courage and strength for the battles of the soul.

* Harper and Brothers, New York, 1949.

Nine The Rediscovery of Man

"The Lord God formed man of the dust of the ground and breathed into his nostrils the breath of life, and man became a living soul." Thus, for many centuries and almost until our own time, western man was accustomed to describe himself and his origins. He had been created complete and innocent at the beginning of the world. He had fallen from innocence and from grace after the pattern of the Genesis myth. It was his ultimate destiny to work, to suffer, to believe, and to hope for the time when he should return again, by divine grace, to the innocence and blessedness which had been his at the morning of the world. History was a decline from original blessedness into original sin and all the consequent sufferings and frustrations. The redemption and the restoration of human nature and of history were to be sought outside history and outside human nature in the power and purpose of God.

Two major insights of the modern world have transformed this view:

The first is that insight into the nature of God which leaves behind the notion of the "Man Upstairs" and conceives God not as a separate super-being above and outside of man, but as the very ground of all being, the underlying source from which all thinking, feeling, purposing, and loving spring. As man's search for God shifts from the effort to find a geographical home for him somewhere in space to the effort to discover God within himself as the foundation of all meaning and all life, he inevitably begins to learn more about himself and to revise his version of himself.

The second major insight which has transformed the old view of man as the fallen angel is a scientific one. Just as the new astronomy destroyed the idea of God as the "Man Upstairs," so the new biology, and in particular the theory of evolution, destroyed the idea of man as descended from a pristine wholeness and innocence. It took billions of years of struggle and growth, of trial and error and emergence, to produce the creature called man. He was not made in a day, and he is not finished yet. Indeed, barring cosmic accidents or the triumph of human stupidity over the human urge to survive and grow, man is in the morning of his day. He is a baby groping towards understanding of himself and of the world. He is only beginning to be aware of what it means to be human and of the challenges and possibilities which surround him. Inevitably, the scientific insight introduced by Darwin and his followers nearly a century ago has compelled modern man to rethink the meaning of his own human nature. This process of the rediscovery of man is not by any means completed. It continues today and will continue for centuries to come. But it has already produced astounding results in man's estimate of himself and his human nature.

We do not have as yet in the modern world a new doctrine of man to take the place of the old one which was lost when the "Man Upstairs" disappeared for thoughtful minds and the myth of the fallen angel died away. What we have so far is a series of partial descriptions and insights, each true enough in its limited way but each capable of terrible distortion and damage when made into a total theory of man and treated as a final truth.

"Man is a rational being." This is one of the many partial descriptions of man in the modern world. It is based upon a sound insight, and it is true as far as it goes. One of the distinctive qualities of man is a capacity for rational thought and reflection upon his experience. The eighteenth and nineteenth centuries set great store by this description of man. Many believed that if man's rational capacities could be fully liberated and fully trained they could lead him to a solution to the besetting problems of his tragic destiny. By reason man could rise triumphant over the perplexities of his existence, set them in order, explain them by cause and effect, and at last remove all mystery and tragedy from the human scene. The rise of the idea of general public education grew out of this faith in man as a rational being, and it has immeasurably deepened and strengthened man's understanding of his world and himself. The obvious fact that man is not in every way a rational being is no excuse for denying that he is in many ways capable of rationality and that reason is one of his most precious capacities. The retreat from reason in our own time was born of disillusionment which came when we began to discover that reason had its limitations as well as its powers. Because reason could not solve all the riddles of existence, millions took the irrational step of thinking that reason was a broken tool which could solve no riddles at all. They began to mistrust the integrity and soundness of their own minds and to scorn the processes of thought itself. They became experts in propaganda, and truth became for them whatever people could be persuaded or compelled to believe. The Nazis revived the ancient practice of burning books as a symbol of the desire to destroy the thoughts which they hated and feared. The Communists, teaching them and learning from them, developed new techniques of destroying ideas and truth by destroying men. They produced the terrible science of brain-washing: the deliberate effort to undermine and finally remove entirely the power of rational thought from living human beings. Even Americans, with their long and honorable tradition of intellectual freedom and respect for reason, have seen, from time to time, a resurgence of dark, irrational emotions of fear and hatred.

The retreat from reason in our time resulted in the reappearance of an old and familiar description of man: "Man is a sinner." The realization that reason did not wholly rule men led many to say that man was, as the Bible and St. Augustine and John Calvin had insisted, infected with some inherent moral sickness. His will was crippled so that he was unable to follow his desire for good. His pride, his self-centeredness, inevitably led to the corruption of his best efforts to follow reason. There is enough truth in this description of man to compel us to take it seriously. All too often we must admit with shame that "we have left undone those things which we ought to have done and have done those things which we ought not to have done." The rediscovery of man as a sinner was a sound corrective to the description of man as an entirely rational being, for the idea of man as a rational being had resulted in another assertion about man: "Man is essentially and inevitably good." This assertion, too, contained some truth. There is something in man that longs for goodness, for love, for the realization of beauty and truth in himself and in the world. In many ways we are all less good than in our hearts we truly want to be. We are aware of high hopes and dreams as well as dark passions and hatreds. But neither the description of man as an original and inevitable sinner nor the description of man as an original and inevitable saint adequately describes man completely. Like the description of man as a rational being, each is true as far as it goes, but neither can be taken as a total description. We are moving today towards a description of man's moral nature which rests neither on original sin nor on original righteousness but, rather, original potentiality for both good and evil. Which of the two wins out in man, we are learning, depends on many factors both within and outside the individual man.

Efforts to explain this process have resulted in further descriptions of man. Each man, some have said, is a free individual. By his thought, his knowledge, and his will power man makes himself what he is and is responsible for all that happens to him. This has been one of the deepest and most fruitful insights of the modern age. It overturned the divine right of kings and the authoritarian church and state. It set men free from slavery of many kinds. It created the idea of democracy and nourished the dreams of equality and brotherhood. Man, it insisted, possessed, merely by virtue of his humanity, a divinely given right to be himself, to express himself, to maintain his own individuality against the encroachments of society and government. This view of man lifted the individual up and gave divinity and meaning to his struggles and hopes. It made him conscious of his inalienable rights and told him that the state and all other human institutions existed for him and for his happiness and welfare. The western world would be poorer in many ways without this description of man as a free being. It is one of the most beautiful and precious things in our heritage; yet, even so, it is not in itself an adequate description of man in his totality. It has had its dark and distorted expressions. The German thinker Nietzsche seized upon this description of man and conceived the idea of the superman, the free soul living beyond good and evil, beyond society, glorying in his strength and answerable to nothing save his own desires and the fulfilment of his own individual being. The diseased mind of Adolph Hitler developed from this the notion of the master race destined to rule all other lesser races by reason of its own inherent superiority and its irresponsible power. There arose the strange anachronism of the supreme infallible ruler, the man who was a father to his people, who knew their needs and provided for them and whose authority was all but divine. It resulted in waves of anti-Semitism and other forms of racial and cultural prejudice whereby little individuals establish to their own satisfaction their inherent and absolute superiority over some other group of people. It resulted in the monstrous illusion that to be free is to be irresponsible, without obligations to truth or to one's fellow human beings, or even to any standard of justice and righteousness beyond one's own desires and needs.

Thus is the great description of man as the free being, the sovereign individual, corrupted and debased unless it is balanced and disciplined by another description: Man is a social animal. The fulfilment of his freedom and his sense of being a unique individual are truly found only as he discovers himself as bound together with other human beings in a family, a community, a nation, or a world-wide brotherhood. He cannot live to himself alone. "No man is an island." There are dangers in this description, too. They are the familiar ones which the totalitarianism and the drive towards conformity in our own age have made so brutally plain. It is possible for the individual to lose himself in the mass, to abandon independent thought, to lose all sense of individual uniqueness and dignity, to become almost an automaton, simply reacting to the social pressures which play upon him, waiting to find out what he thinks or wants until he hears what he is supposed to think and want. When men do thus lose themselves in the mass, terrible things happen. Individual conscience and the feeling of personal moral responsibility die away. A man can commit all kinds of crimes against his fellow human beings simply because he is ordered to do so or because the safety of the nation requires it. He is a criminal if he harms a single member of his own group but a hero if he helps destroy millions of aliens or outsiders. He has become so completely a social animal that he has lost his own soul and his own sense of individuality.

The two descriptions of man as a sovereign and free individual and as a social animal must always be taken together. When either one is pressed to its ultimate conclusion without the other, it results in a degradation of man himself. Yet each is true as far as it goes and in its own way, and each is important to a total description of man.

Another description of man has been very powerful in our age. "Man is an economic animal." The real conflict between communism and the free world is not really a conflict between materialism and a spiritual view of life. It is a conflict between two materialisms: two civilizations, each of which believes essentially that man's basic problem is the organization and distribution of material goods. We have tried to solve this problem within the framework of freedom for the individual and, consequently, we have left wide spaces for other than material fulfilments. Communism has tried to solve it by terror and violence and by a fixed dogma of man as a social and economic animal and nothing more. Of course, it is true that man is an economic animal; that the satisfaction of his material needs for bread and security is essential to any other kind of satisfaction life may hold. The statement that "man does not live by bread alone" does not mean that man does not need bread in order to live. But we must put the description of man as an economic animal in its proper perspective. Man lives by bread plus: bread plus love, plus joy, plus beauty, plus hope and faith. Perhaps the resolution of the present world tension will come when the two great civilizations involved with their opposing ways of social organization begin to make provision for the non-economic necessities and satisfactions of human life, and in so doing enlarge their vision of man as a being who is both material and spiritual, both body and something else and more which we may call "soul." At any rate, it seems likely that the issue cannot be resolved by the triumph of one form of materialism over another but, rather, by the appearance within our civilization of new ways of thinking about man which open up wider possibilities for him than any which the dogma of economic man alone can ever provide.

Other descriptions of man have crowded in upon us in recent years. Man is in some measure, perhaps a larger one than we realize, the result of his inheritance, his genes. And man is the result of the social-cultural patterns into which he is born and in the midst of which he grows up. They shape him and form his opinions, his likes and dislikes, his hopes and dreams and even his faith. Man is the creature of deep, dark impulses within his own nature: his subconscious sexual drives, his will to power, or the collective unconscious of the race stored up within him beneath the floor of memory and conscious understanding. He is a combination of conditioned reflexes, a cluster of instincts and drives, a product of environment in home and community, a prey to massive historical forces which carry him along with them.

In some way or other and to some degree, all these descriptions are true. The one great block to an adequate understanding of man and a deep appreciation of his possibilities and his problems is our all too human tendency to take one or two of these descriptions and erect them into a theory of man which claims to be final and complete. Man is the creature of all these forces, but of no one or two or three of them alone. The great fact about man is his complexity, his many-sidedness, the infinite variety of possibilities, meanings, and energies. It may not be literally true in the old mythical sense that man is properly described as the "child of God." But it is certainly true that in man are met all the mysteries, meanings, potentialities, and tragedies which surround and underlie our life. It is man who feels them, tries, often in vain, to understand them, and endlessly labors to express in his own life and the lives of others the infinite creativeness out of which he emerged and of which he is a part.

One thing we can be sure of: Any description of man which reduces him simply to the status of a pawn, driven and controlled entirely by inner or outer forces which are beyond his comprehension or his power to change, will be inadequate. It may be true as far as it goes, but it does not go all the way to the reality which is man. Just when you think you have him neatly explained and have worked out a set of answers he produces the fresh, the creative, the surprising thing, the thing which could never have been predicted from all that you thought you knew about him.

The more one ponders the problem the more it seems that the ancient, poetic, religious descriptions of man convey authentic hints of the mysterious truth. He is "a little lower than the angels" and a little higher than the beasts. He is the "dust of the ground" into which somehow the breath of life, the creative spark, the living soul have been infused. The potentialities within him run all the way from Jesus Christ or the Buddha to the very worst human degradation that we have seen or imagined. Somewhere within him there must be a flame of holy freedom, with all its attendant terrors and glories. Somewhere within man there lives and works a power and meaning which is not man but more than man, which is akin to man, connected with him as the tiny stream is connected with the great ocean and the single drop of water with the stream.

The rediscovery of man in our day will be incomplete unless it takes into account this dimension of depth within the human spirit. There is something in man that partakes of and responds to the ultimate mystery which is at the foundation of all existence. Man does not know the answer to the mystery. He is only dimly aware that it is there and that he is part of it. He is the one who contemplates the mystery, and he is himself a part of the mystery which he contemplates. Man is a strange, double being: human and yet divine, not God, yet made in the image of God. The task of the religious spirit in furthering the rediscovery of man is to encourage man to see himself truly as a being still in process of growth and development, full of possibility in spite of his limitations, a creature who has traveled far and still has far to go.

Ten A New Age of Reason

A genuine awakening of religion in our time will be accompanied by a renewed awareness of the importance of knowledge and of rational thought. Historians have called the eighteenth century the age of reason. The struggle for human liberty which took place in that period both in Europe and America was led by men who had perceived that in the power of thought and the ability to accumulate and interpret knowledge man possessed a pair of powerful tools with which to better his own condition. They also perceived that these tools could not be effectively used except in an atmosphere of freedom. Man must be free to think and to express his thoughts without fear and to exchange ideas with other men. That freedom could not be restricted to the privileged few. It must be made available to the many. The great thinkers of the age of reason in Europe, men like Voltaire, Diderot, and Rousseau; the Founding Fathers in America: Jefferson, Paine, Adams, and the rest, insisted that all men possessed the power of rational thought and could, if only they were free from tyranny and arbitrary interference, use that power together for their mutual benefit. Never was a more sublime faith expressed and acted upon in history. The foundations of American freedom are in the conviction that if men are truly free they can be trusted in the long run to make the choices which will be of mutual benefit to all. Some of the Founding Fathers, notably Alexander Hamilton, feared this faith. They did not dare trust the minds and consciences of ordinary people that much. But after more than a century and a half of historical experience it now seems clear that the society which carefully guards the rights of individuals, encourages rational thought among its citizens, tries earnestly to spread among them knowledge of their common affairs, respects their varied opinions and desires is a stronger, more creative, more resilient society than one which is directed by the authority of a few—no matter how competent, well-informed and well-intentioned those few may be.

The nineteenth century has been called the age of invention. To the power of reason and freedom were added the fruits of man's inventiveness and technical skill. So great were the transformations of man's life wrought in that age, so wonderful and useful were its achievements that by the end of the nineteenth century most Americans had accepted a very rosy view of their history and their destiny. There seemed to be no reason why progress should not go forward, "onward and upward forever." The combination of increasing technical skills and their resultant material benefits and the spread of education and the application of rational principles to human affairs must, it seemed, inevitably result in the conquest of the age-old problems of poverty and bigotry and disease and war, and the eventual emergence of the kingdom of God on earth.

But it was not to be so. Certain dark, uncontrolled, destructive impulses and desires in human nature had been left out of account in this rosy view of human destiny. When Lord Grey, the British Prime Minister, said in the summer of 1914 as the First World War began, "The Lights are going out all over Europe tonight," he prophesied more truly than he knew. The light of reason was going out to burn again only fitfully and in isolated places for many years to come. It was all but overwhelmed in the hatreds, cruelties and fears generated by the First World War. It flared up only to die down again in Woodrow Wilson's heroic attempt to create a structure for the creation and preservation of peace and in the inability of the great powers, including the United States, to take the necessary steps towards forming a world organization strong enough to keep the peace. The light of freedom and reason died out as the Communist tyranny gripped the people of Russia and sought to spread across the world, and as Hitler's Nazis in Germany erected a structure of cruelty and hatred, persecuted Jews and foreigners, burned books, suppressed thought, and prepared their plans for conquest of the world. The Second World War engulfed the whole world in a struggle so vast and so bitter that the voice of reason could hardly be heard; and the years since the war have seen, here in America, the pathological hatred and fear of communism seriously threaten the liberties of millions of Americans. This hatred and fear have carried some Americans to the point where they regard thinking itself as a danger to the nation and non-conformity as a crime. The intellectual, the thinker, the "egghead" became an object of ridicule and suspicion. All in all, the first half of the twentieth century represents a continuation of the age of invention on a scale grander than ever before, but an abrupt break with the age of reason and the rise of a cult of irrationality which has placed consecrated ignorance above rational thought and fanatical partisanship above the search for truth and justice in human affairs.

The end of this process was suggested by George Orwell in his terrifying novel *1984*. Orwell pictures a civilization enormously efficient in a technical sense, where private thinking has become a crime. The distinction between truth and falsehood has been utterly obliterated by the omnipotent, omnipresent state. Not only the present and the future but even the past are in the control of the "Ministry of Truth." Past events which do not fit in with present theories and plans are expunged from the record, and new records are created to establish "true" history. The book is a fantasy, of course, but not so fantastic that one cannot see suggestions of the process in contemporary events. The transformation of Joseph Stalin from the position of Father, Deliverer, Savior of the Russian people to Traitor, Tyrant and Devil Incarnate is an example of what determined, opportunistic men who have no respect for truth, reason, freedom, or thought can do about re-creating the past in the image which is convenient for the present. We have learned in this century that the minds of men can be compelled to abandon thought and reason entirely and to believe, with all their hearts, that two plus two equal five or three or whatever the State says. When there is no accepted standard of truth, no test whereby truth can be determined, whoever has power makes his own truth and forces it upon the people.

The light of reason has burned fitfully during the first half of the twentieth century, but at least it has burned here and there. One of the signs of an authentic awakening of religion will be our recovery as a people from succeeding spasms of irrational fear and hatred and our recovery of respect for the roles which thought and reason play in our common life. For, while it is true that reason has its limitations and that we live not only by rational thought but by deep emotional drives and hungers within the human heart, it is also true that blind impulses, emotional shock treatments, irrational loves, fears, and hatreds are no substitutes for the orderly processes of thought and can lead us, unless they are tested and disciplined by reason, into loss of freedom, of objectivity and even of sanity.

It is notable that in spite of the widespread popular emphasis on peace of mind and the pieties of patriotism and of emotional shock treatment, there is a growing concern with religion as a field of knowledge and thought with which any intelligent person should be reasonably familiar. My experience over a number of years with students on numerous college campuses suggests to me that the current "revival of religion" is not so much a vast increase in the number of "decisions for Christ" as it is a genuine desire among many students to find abiding meanings in life, and a new willingness to study thoughtfully the religious traditions of mankind in search of those meanings. It is not without significance that Harvard University in the past five years has re-established its

Divinity School, one of the oldest in the nation, on new foundations, greatly expanding its size and scope, and has found widespread public interest and support for this enterprise. Churches and foundations are now actively engaged in trying to find outstanding young men for the profession of the ministry and are willing to spend much time and money to make sure that the clergy in years to come shall be competent, learned, and well-prepared for the complicated tasks of the Christian minister. Gone are the days, at least in the major denominations, when an attractive fellow with strong lungs, a glib tongue, and some political know-how can establish himself as a minister of religion. The major denominations today are deeply concerned that their churches be served not only by sincere, well-meaning men, but by competent, well-educated men. And this new emphasis is a kind of reawakening.

For in the early days of America religion and learning went hand in hand. Many of our finest colleges and universities were founded by religious men with the express purpose of providing the churches with a "learned ministry." The minister in many a colonial community was often the most learned, if not the only learned, man in town; and he spoke with authority not only on the Bible and the Faith but on law, history, philosophy, and government. The clergyman today holds no such position of intellectual eminence. No matter how well-trained and studious he may be there will be many fields of learning in which his knowledge is very slight. The age of reason in the eighteenth century was probably the last time in history that a reasonably intelligent and industrious man could feel at home discussing almost any subject. He might not be an expert, but the field of knowledge was small enough so that at least he could know what the experts were talking about. Today the field of human knowledge is so vast that nobody can know enough to converse intelligently in all of it. He must rely on the experts and use his intuitions as to the reliability and sincerity of what they say. A former teacher of mine used to tell the story of the day when he was asked to be Dean of the Divinity

School of a great university. At the time he was a parish minister and keenly felt his lack of expert training in any of the fields which as Dean he would have to supervise. "Mr. President," he protested to the president of the university, "I am not a scholar." The president replied: "You don't have to be a scholar. All you have to do is know one when you see one." And that is about all that most of us can do today. Except in a very limited area our knowledge is bound to be sketchy and superficial. But we can and must learn to recognize the ring of truth when we hear it.

In almost every aspect of human life today, the expert reigns supreme. This is as it should be. He has taken the time and trouble to inform himself as thoroughly as possible on the facts and the techniques in a particular field. We defer to him naturally when he speaks as an expert. We would not dream as laymen of arguing with a surgeon who was about to perform an operation about the necessity of the operation or the manner in which it should be performed. That is his profession, and we simply entrust ourselves to his hands, accepting the fact of his superior knowledge and experience. Nor would we as laymen argue with the lawyer, the physicist, the mathematician, the biologist, or the specialist in any field. We assume that he knows what he is doing and that in all such areas you do not have any competence to express an opinion unless you are familiar with the basic principles involved and have some working knowledge of how they are applied to actual cases. But in the field of religion, at least theoretically, anyone's opinion is as true and as valuable as anyone else's. The simple, untutored, natural man may have an experience of God more profound and more vital than the man who has spent his whole life amassing data as to the nature of religious experience. Indeed, there is a strong bias in Christianity against the intellectual approach to religion. Jesus said that in order to inherit the Kingdom of Heaven we must become as little children and many have warned against the dangers of losing oneself in the pursuit of mere knowledge about religion and thereby missing the simplicity and directness of religious experience itself.

True as this is, it must be remembered that religion also is a field of knowledge. This is especially so for the two connected historical religions which make up the spiritual heritage of the western world: Judaism and Christianity. Christianity is the child of Judaism. "Spiritually," said the Pope, "we are all Semites." Four thousand years of constant change, development, interpretation of ideas, and application of faith to historical challenges have gone into the making of the Judeo-Christian religious heritage which is ours. It would seem obvious that you cannot grasp the significance of this long tradition today if you approach it in almost total ignorance of the experience of the past. Yet, I fear that this is what many people are doing. They desire the sense of meaning and purpose, of peace and of power which is associated with the profoundest kind of religious experience. But often they do not have enough knowledge of what men have experienced as religion to know whether their own experience is religious or not. A young man, a senior in one of our great universities, a man on the way to competent scholarship in the scientific disciplines, said to me once: "I am ashamed of myself. I honestly do not know what happened in the history of Christianity from the Letters of St. Paul to the founding of the first Unitarian Church of San Francisco. If I were as ignorant as that in any of the fields in which I am studying at the University, I would flunk out and deserve to."

I do not mean to suggest that in order to find a living religious faith everyone must become a scholar and a specialist in Christian history and the development of Christian thought and theology. But it is not impossible for a thoughtful and intelligent person, by reading two or three basic books, to gain an adequate working knowledge of what Christianity is, how it came into being and how it developed into what it is today. Our laws compel every new American to take a course in Americanism during which he reads such basic documents as the Declaration of Independence and the Constitution and becomes familiar with the language, the customs, and the basic principles of American life. Is it unthinkable that a man who is genuinely interested in religion might feel it necessary to read the basic source book of the Judeo-Christian faith, the Bible, and with the aid of a simple and competent commentary—of which there are many—to find out how it was written, what its basic story is, and what it means in the light of the development of his own religion today? Many people might have much more respect for religion if it were presented not as "helpful hints for daily living" nor as some vague and mysterious sort of experience which you drop into church and have of a Sunday morning, but as a serious, persistent, and important concern of thoughtful people from generation to generation. In many ways, we have made religion too easy to "get," forgetting that in religion as in any other important interest of man the price of finding real satisfaction and fulfilment is careful thought and patient persistence in the effort to understand. Religion must be presented in such a way that the thoughtful and learned person in any field can respect it and use the same skills that he uses in the quest for truth and understanding in any other field. We must get away from that definition of faith which was reputedly given by the down-east farmer: "Faith is believing something that you know ain't so." The quest of religion is a quest for intellectual integrity and completeness. Our religious convictions will differ and may often carry us beyond reason and that which can be rationally proven. But if our thinking is sound, those convictions will not contradict what we have found to be true anywhere.

One refreshing sign of a renewed interest in religion on a thoughtful, rational basis is the fact that not only in colleges and universities—among the eggheads as it were—but also among ordinary laymen there is today a growing willingness to think seriously about the great religious questions: What is God? What is Man? What is evil?

What is salvation? What is truth? What is Eternal Life? These questions have perennially perplexed and challenged the minds of men. They are in final terms unanswerable, and yet we cannot leave them alone. And the anxious age has compelled many people to re-state them with renewed urgency. In my own experience as a parish minister, it has seemed to me that most people are much more interested in discussing these questions than in the more tangible ones of an international, political, social, or economic nature. Some people, it is true, are content to leave these questions out of their consideration on the grounds that they are impossible of resolution anyhow, but there are many who have the same attitude towards them that Charles Leigh Mallory had towards the conquest of Mt. Everest in which he lost his life. When someone asked him why he wanted to climb Mt. Everest, he replied: "I want to climb the mountain because it is there." For increasing numbers of people, these questions are there. They ask themselves. Life compels us to raise them. And so, even though they are finally unanswerable, man will continue to ponder them, for they will exert the fascination upon him that the then unclimbed Everest exerted upon Mallory and the others who sought to climb it.

In one church with which I am familiar, a group of some sixty people, without any previous coaching from the minister, decided that they would undertake to spend a year of thoughtful study on a single one of the great religious questions: What is Man? Carefully and patiently they began looking at this question from many different points of view and from the perspective of the many different answers which have been offered. They examined the creation stories in the Bible. They examined the idea of evolution. They talked with biologists, anthropologists, sociologists, psychologists. They studied what other great religions of mankind have had to say on the subject. They did not arrive at a simple and neatly-phrased answer to the question, but their minds were greatly expanded and deepened by the process of considering it together. It is possibly a sign of a deeper awakening of religion in our time that you are no longer considered queer if you want to discuss such questions. It is understood that thoughtful people can and must discuss them as part of the search for meaning in their own lives.

In all our thinking about religion, we must keep in mind the subtle and close relationship between reason and emotion, between thought and feeling. Try as we will, we can never really separate these two elements which go into our beliefs. For purposes of analysis, there may be such a thing as "pure reason," but in life all reason is tinged with emotion, and all emotion, at least among the sane, is in some measure disciplined and directed by reason and thought. Religion has often been regarded as an area where emotion and faith reign as against reason and thought. But religion is also the effort to make sense out of life, to grapple with its mysteries, to think one's way through to some kind of solid ground. Yet in all our thinking, there are elements of need, desire, longing, and love. We cannot keep them out, and we would be dead if we succeeded in keeping them out. We should not be ashamed of these elements or reject them. Feeling is the force which enables us to act upon thought, to bring ideas over into the field of action. The man of pure reason, if he existed, might be a very wise and knowledgeable fellow, but he would be quite incapable of action since he would be continually halting between two opinions, each of which was as rational as the other. In the long run, it is what we care for, what we love, what "feels right" that enables us to act creatively. The religious task is to feel thoughtfully and to think feelingly.

We come to our deepest beliefs not because they are rational and consistent throughout but because, having followed the pathway of reason as far as it goes, we are led to take a further step by some inner need and love which whispers: "It could be so." For example, no man really knows—and it is beyond the reach of thought even to imagine—what awaits us on the other side of the gates of death: perhaps nothing, perhaps anything. We do not know, and it is better frankly to say so. But sometimes a man can feel in the very depths of his soul the mystery and the possibility suggested in the lines from Whittier's hymn "Who Fathoms the Eternal Thought":

> I know not where His islands lift
> Their fronded palms in air;
> I only know I cannot drift
> Beyond His love and care.

Such faith is made up of both thought and feeling. It does not presume, as religion often has, to describe in precise language the outlines of the heavenly geography or the personal and social conditions of life in eternity. It does affirm man's abiding intuition that there are more things in heaven and earth than are dreamt of in his philosophy, and man's stubborn intuition of being related somehow to that which is eternal. Religious thought, whether it be directed towards the ultimate questions of God, Man, Eternity, Salvation or towards the more worldly question of justice, mercy, truth, and love as conditions to be created on this earth, is inevitably suffused with emotion. There is always present the longing to see in the midst of life that which has hitherto existed only in the hopes and dreams of men. That longing is never entirely fulfilled, but it is the force which makes thought creative. Always the effort of thought must be made, for where it is not made, man brings to the religious quest not his whole self nor even the best part of himself but his crude desire for comfort or peace of mind or certainty at any price, even the price of the integrity of his own mind.

One of the perils of thought, especially common in the western world, is the tendency to confuse words and ideas with truth and reality. The long and tragic record of Christian exclusiveness, bigotry, and persecution arises from the persistent habit of supposing that when you have formulated a belief in words and won verbal consent to it you have established that belief. When Galileo reported his observations of the movements of the sun and the earth and his speculation that the earth did move around the sun, it caused consternation among the churchmen whose whole theology rested upon the belief that the earth was a fixed body at the center of the universe. They reacted characteristically. They took Galileo into the dungeons of the Inquisition, and they showed him the instruments of torture there and asked him if he thought the earth moved or not. Galileo was old and tired. He could not face the pain which he knew would come if he did not comply with their wishes. And so he denied the observations which he had made with his own eyes and his own mind and was duly repentant for his sin. But under his breath it is said that he whispered, "And yet it does move, it does move." The priests supposed that because they had secured a verbal denial from Galileo they had established the nature of the universe as they wanted it to be. But of course, they had done nothing of the sort. The truth was not affected by what they said or by what Galileo said. It was the truth. We persist in thinking, for example, that God is a word, a concept, a theory to be argued about rather than the name for a profound kind of human experience, a continuing activity in the world, a sense of meaning and confidence within the human heart which millions of persons actually do feel whether they use the word or not. What is needed is a way of thinking about religion which will illuminate human experiences of grandeur, wonder, commitment, and love without tying those experiences to fixed verbal formulae. A word is not the thing or the experience. It only stands for them. Too often in religion the word has been present and has been spoken, but the thing itself, the experience, has been absent.

The task of thought in religion is to help clear away the rubbish of formal words and stale ideas and understand the meaning of what happens to us in fresh and original ways. Religion is renewed in every generation by those who have the courage, the patience, and the intellectual integrity to look beneath the verbal formulae which have been passed on from the past and see them in terms of the living experience of men and women.

The new age of reason will not be like the eighteenth century. It will exhibit a renewed respect for rational thinking and for the dignity of thought, but it will lack the eighteenth century's certainty that reason is the key to all mysteries and all knowledge. We know, as our forefathers did not, that there are powerful, irrational forces at work within men and their societies and that these forces have much to do with what happens within and among men. Reason will be seen not as the only tool wherewith man can understand himself and his world. But it will still be an essential tool, perhaps the tool without which these ends cannot be achieved. We were right to leave behind the sterile rationalism which dared not think of a world which was not entirely orderly, rational, and amenable to explanation by the mind of man. But we were wrong to conclude that because this was so, reason and the life of thought had no relevance at all. We were wrong to suppose that we could safely live and survive by merely reacting emotionally to the things that happened. We were wrong to think of religion as nothing more than the repetition of glib verbal formulae, the losing of the self in mass movements of a patriotic or revivalistic nature, the achievement of satisfying emotional experiences. Religion may and probably does include some of these things, but it is also man's sober and patient effort to understand himself and his world, using all the powers of mind which are at his command. Sanity and a new birth of religious insight will return when we recover this important truth, gain new respect for the freedom and creative power of the human mind in action, and recognize reason as a sacred and creative flame.

Eleven Religion and Mental Health

This, as we have been often told, is the age of the "organization man," the "outer-directed" man, the "member of the team." The individual, particularly in our large cities, struggles to preserve his sense of identity and individuality. His ideas and opinions are provided for him ready-made by the mass media. His areas of free choice are limited by economic demands, social prejudices, and the precise definition of his limited responsibility which is found in his job description. Few and fortunate are those who work for themselves and have real freedom of thought and expression. But often those few are regarded by the mass as oddities, eccentric and perhaps dangerous and subversive. It has never been easy to be a free man. But today it is harder than ever, not because we live under a tyranny, but because the very abundance of our conveniences and the complexity of the scheme of things into which we must somehow fit ourselves tend to blind us to the basic simplicities of freedom and responsibility.

Even religion, which has often been a powerful force in support of personal freedom and individuality is, in its best-known expressions, mass-produced, mass-publicized, mass-marketed. The abiding impression of the Billy Graham revival in New York's Madison Square Garden is not the ideas expressed, nor the depth and beauty of the Christian religion, but the smoothness, efficiency, and technical excellence of the performance itself. *Variety,* quite correctly, reviewed one of these meetings as a stage performance and found it flawless both as to the star, the supporting cast, and the stage settings. As a spectacle, the Graham meetings were unforgettable:

the vast auditorium packed to the ceiling, the massed choir, the dynamic and impeccable Dr. Graham, the decision makers coming meekly forward and being herded through the doors into the anterooms by the ushers; all this is perfect. But is it religion?

Peace of mind is likewise dispensed by highly efficient means. Buy *The Power of Positive Thinking* and it will tell you just what to do when that wave of discouragement overwhelms you. Or dial a number on the phone and a suave voice will reply with a canned message of hope and comfort. Or if you prefer and have a hi-fi machine, you can write to an organization called *Relax* and they will send you a record which is claimed to have the power to assuage your grief, strengthen your weakness, and put you to sleep soundly. It is all very wonderful, very streamlined, very modern, but it has little if anything to do with religion and certainly nothing to do with the religion of Jesus of Nazareth.

One of the great central Christian themes is expressed beautifully in the Epistle to the Hebrews: "These all died in faith, not having received the promises, but having seen them afar off, and were persuaded of them and embraced them and confessed that they were strangers and pilgrims on the earth." Jesus and his disciples, the apostles and builders of the Christian church, and the church itself in its days of greatness and creative love made religion beautiful and alluring because they knew themselves to be strangers and pilgrims on the earth, because they stood against the world as it was, because they pointed to a better country. They were not well-adjusted to the world they knew. They did not function smoothly in the structure of society which produced them. They were pioneers and discoverers who urged the construction of a new and better world in the midst of the old one. Jesus was crucified and Paul died a prisoner and the early Christians suffered persecution and were fed to lions. It was not a group of wicked men who brought these things about. It was the official system of government and custom and tradition and religion which destroyed them because they challenged it, exposed its hypocrisies, and refused stubbornly to become well adjusted.

I do not detect this note of adventure, this pilgrim spirit either in the revivalism of Dr. Graham or the peace of mind offered by Dr. Peale and others. Either path leads men not into new freedom and selfhood, but deeper into the pattern of conformity. Organization men in their jobs and in their opinions and in their activities, many tend to become organization men in religion as well.

I will admit that in the process perhaps some kinds of anxieties are healed or at least somewhat assuaged. I am sure life does not hurt so much for a while after you have made a decision for Christ at Madison Square Garden or followed the book's instructions about what to do when you are worried. And in a world of much pain and tragedy perhaps any reduction of suffering must be called a net gain. But neither does life hurt so much after you have swallowed a tranquilizer or had that next drink or taken your sleeping pill. The trouble is that all these remedies wear off and have to be taken again and again to achieve the state of euphoria which is desired. The anxieties which gave rise to the pain are not resolved or removed. They are simply blunted for the time being and they return with renewed vigor. The medical profession is becoming seriously concerned about the number of tranquilizers which normal Americans swallow each year. They are even raising the question of whether it is in the interest of health to assuage normal anxiety. They suggest that a certain amount of anxiety may be essential to creative living.

We must have a new definition of what constitutes mental health and mental illness. Mental health is not smooth adjustment to the world as it is. Religion is not a force for conformity. Religion, and especially Christianity, is a revolutionary power which makes one profoundly aware of the integrity of one's own soul, of the obligations which the fact of one's freedom and one's individuality place upon one, of the necessity for growth and change in oneself and in the world. Mental health is a state of being in which a man sees himself truly, uses his powers creatively, is capable of steady loyalty and patience and love, and, in the words of the familiar prayer, accepts what cannot be changed, changes what can be changed, and knows the one from the other.

Religion and psychology today have similar goals: the development of the individual into a free, creative, responsible person and a constructive member of the community. The mutual suspicion which used to prevail in the relationships between clergymen and doctors or psychiatrists has all but disappeared. The major theological schools today, both Catholic and Protestant, make sure that the men they are preparing for priesthood or ministry have a sound introduction to the basic principles of psychology and their importance in the clergyman's task as a healer of souls. Doctors and psychiatrists co-operate in this kind of education and in a few places medical students are being exposed to the fact that the religious attitudes of the people whom they will be treating as patients will play a vital part in their health. There is no longer warfare between religion and psychology. Rather in many places there is a serious experimental effort to bring together the two approaches to life and encourage their fruitful interplay.

This co-operative approach has already yielded some interesting discoveries. For example, some forms of religion are distinctly neurotic manifestations. The person who carries about with him a compulsive sense of guilt so that the smallest mistakes and errors of judgement are in his eye magnified into grievous sins is not religious. He is sick. Or again, the person of hard and closed mind, who has adopted a set of unyielding dogmas by which he judges all persons and events and from which he will not deviate even in the presence of new knowledge, is simply bigoted and unable to do what is characteristic of the healthy human mind: to move hopefully from the truth he has found so far to the richer truth which enlarged knowledge and deeper experience make possible.

But surely the most important fruit of the interplay between religion and psychology has been a new picture of the meaning of mental health and religiousness. We once thought that the religious man was one who, protected by his firm faith and his fixed doctrines, set himself apart from the ways of the wicked world. And we once thought that the mentally healthy person was just the opposite: one who, having accepted the world and its ways, adjusted himself to them and learned to function as successfully as possible. It is now plain that each of these definitions was only partly true and that each is inadequate without the tempering influence of the other. Both clergymen and psychiatrists would now agree that the healthy person combines in himself both of these characteristics. He is the free individual who lives by his own ideas and convictions and functions usefully and creatively in society.

It is interesting that in primitive communities the pattern of conformity is the same, though not so complex, as the pattern of conformity which rules so much our life today. In primitive societies the community makes the man. From the cradle to the grave his life is governed and surrounded by the customs and taboos of the tribe. They support and shape the life of the individual, and breaking with custom is a serious crime which threatens the security of the whole society. Religion in such societies is little more than the dramatization in ritual of the prevailing customs of the tribe.

In more advanced societies the individual begins to have a sense of his own personal meaning and destiny. He experiences a kinship with God which is not communal but intimate and personal. He sees himself as a member of the community but also as a distinct person set apart from the community. He begins to think his own thoughts and make his own choices. Sometimes those thoughts and choices run counter to prevailing custom and tradition. The free individual is a fruit of civilization. The ideal of the noble savage is a delusion. Both religion and psychology seek to stimulate the growth of this free individual, to help him express himself and to create the social conditions within which he will have a chance to make his influence felt. The real test of a person's health, for both religion and psychology, is not how well he conforms to the tribal or communal pattern but the degree of positive individuality he has achieved and the degree of responsibility and constructive love with which he exercises his personal freedom. In the same way the test of a society or a civilization's health is the number and quality of the genuinely free persons it is producing. Religion is a creative transforming force and psychology is a science which, by enabling man to understand himself better, helps to set free the creative powers which are in his own mind and heart. What we seek in both religion and psychology is not the skill to conform but the power to transform. St. Paul put it well: "Be not conformed to this world, but be ye transformed by the renewing of your minds that ye may prove what is that good and perfect and acceptable will of God."

We have in recent years spent much time and effort in the attempt to analyze and define the various types of mental illness which have become all too common in the modern world and which seem to arise out of the manifold pressures and anxieties of contemporary civilization. Immensely valuable as this effort has been I want to attempt another approach to the problem here and try to set forth some of the characteristics which might be associated with mental health and a sound religious view. The profile of a healthy religious person may help us to see some of the deficiencies in our own lives and some of the goals towards which we might strive.

The healthy religious person has discovered a framework of meaning, both theological and humanistic, within which he is able to judge and evaluate the more specific meanings and choices of his own life. He has a worldview. It is not fixed and closed; there is room in it for growth and change. But it does provide him with standards for judgement so that the incessant demands and challenges of life can be met and decided in somewhat orderly fashion. He is not wandering or drifting aimlessly.

He has a sense of direction. This framework of meaning and sense of direction may be expressed in religious doctrines or it may be much more informal. Franz Werfel in his preface to his novel *The Song of Bernadette* sets forth his own framework of meaning in these words: "Even in the days when I wrote my first verses I resolved that I would evermore glorify and uphold the divine mystery and holiness in man, careless of an age which has turned with scorn and anger from the ultimate values of our human lot." Ours is an age when many have lost any real sense of meaning in their lives. Having no meaning in themselves, they find none in the world around them and so become the prey to any articulate person or group which is sure enough of itself to speak with conviction. The beginning of health is the discovery of meaning within the self.

The healthy religious person is in touch with reality. He is not chasing rainbows. He is not preoccupied with Utopia. He has come to see that growth and improvement in himself or others or the world cannot come into being except from the condition of things as they are. William Temple, the late Archbishop of Canterbury, once remarked that if by some miracle the laws and patterns of a genuinely Christian society could be established, we would wreck that society within a fortnight since we ourselves are not yet sufficiently mature in our Christianity to be able to make it work. The healthy religious person has abandoned his illusions of perfection. He is concerned with growth, with the long and painful effort to make himself and the world a little better. How often it has seemed to me that a more modest idealism might save us endless frustration over the failure of our best ideals to find concrete realization in the world and at the same time enable us to find some proper satisfaction in the fact that with the passing years and centuries some good and abiding achievements have been made. As one watches with awe the desperate struggle in the South to win for all its people the equality of opportunity and brotherhood which are part of the American dream and rooted in the Christian vision of the kingdom of God, one is more and more impressed not with the zealots and absolutists on either side of the struggle but with the crying need for people who know it is a long long job requiring infinite patience, firmness, tact, and mutual respect. This combination of courage and realism, of idealism and understanding, is characteristic of the healthy religious person. His faith and idealism are tempered and actually strengthened by what has been called "the discipline of the possible."

The healthy religious person makes a fetish neither of conformity nor of non-conformity. Many people today, as we have seen, seek nothing but conformity. They are horrified at the idea of standing out from the crowd. They want nothing but to live their lives as smoothly and unobtrusively as possible, yielding to pressures which play upon them, adjusting themselves as smoothly as possible to the world as it is. Some few, however, seek nothing but non-conformity. They are unhappy if they find themselves on the side of the majority. They think there must be something wrong with them, some lack of courage and integrity if they find themselves agreeing with anyone. They are chronic rebels and come-outers. Both groups have lost their freedom and their individuality. The conformists have lost out because they dare say or do nothing save what public opinion approves and dictates. The non-conformists have lost out because they are by some inner compulsion driven to do the opposite. The chronic conformist is a cipher. The chronic non-conformist can all too easily become an embittered crackpot. For sometimes what the majority approves and dictates is right. If it were not we could not make democracy work at all. The healthy religious person is one who guards his own integrity and freedom of judgement and makes his own choices out of the best knowledge and insight of his own mind and heart plus what he can learn from others.

The healthy religious person sees life as a journey. He knows that he is a pilgrim, that the successive generations of men are on a long pilgrimage from the known and the familiar out into the unknown and the new. His eyes are not turned backward wistfully towards a past which has been left behind nor forward with wild longing towards a beautiful future which he cannot hope to see realized in his day. He moves and works in the living present in the faith that the new emerges out of the old. The Christian faith, whether orthodox or liberal, has always seen man as a temporary citizen, a traveler through the world that is. Sometimes the journey has been described as a journey towards heaven, sometimes as a process whereby the Kingdom of God is to be realized in the world. But always man is a wayfarer, who may not stop and rest for long. The healthy religious person sees the process of life as Thomas Wolfe describes it in the closing lines of his great novel *You Can't Go Home Again*:

> To lose the earth you know for greater knowing; to lose the life you have for greater life; to leave the friends you loved for greater loving; to find a land more kind than home, more large than earth whereon the pillars of this earth are founded; towards which the conscience of the world is tending: a wind is rising and the rivers flow.

The healthy religious person finds his peace of mind and refreshment of spirit in the joy and zest of the work he has undertaken, in the companionship of kindred souls in the religious community whose struggles and adventures he shares. The special strength of the church is that it is, at best, a community of seekers. Each person brings to it his own best insights and skills. He shares them with others, teaching them and learning from their stores of knowledge and experience. The church upholds the individual in his times of strain and uncertainty. It is the supporting fellowship of those who share the values for which he works. Because the church is there he is able to do better than he could hope to do alone. It may be that there are great solitary saints whose spirits burn with such a bright clear flame and whose insights are so far ahead of those which ordinary men can share that they do not need the support of the religious community and indeed find it a hindrance rather than a help. But most of us are not saints and do need and depend on the support which can come from the community of like-minded men and women. The church is not a fellowship of saints. It is a fellowship of ordinary men and women who know all too well that they are not saints but wish at least to be somewhat better than they are. The healthy religious person is one who has learned how to be a humble member of such a fellowship, to contribute what he can to its common life, and to draw strength from it in his own times of need.

It is interesting to speculate what will become of the thousands of persons who under Billy Graham's urging have made "decisions for Christ." If they were, as many were, already churchmen and women, that is one thing. But if they were not, it is a far cry from a mass-meeting in Madison Square Garden with its spotlights, its television cameras, its thrilling massed choirs, and its dynamic and handsome evangelist, to the workaday life of an ordinary church. Here there is little glamor and excitement. No minister can be thrilling and inspiring Sunday after Sunday. There is much hard work to do all the way from raising money, which comes hard, to teaching a class, sitting on a committee, working in an organization, helping others in distress. It is not always fun and nobody always feels inspired. But the tasks of the church must go on, and minister and people must carry them out no matter how they feel at any given moment. The real challenge to the new converts will come later when there is basketball and prize fighting in Madison Square Garden, and the converts are confronted with the sober necessities of life in a continuing church. The healthy religious person is one who has learned to carry his share of these burdens from day to day. He has grasped the significance of Jesus' words when he said: "Nevertheless I must walk today, tomorrow and the day following."

The healthy religious person has a realistic attitude towards the tribulation that is in the world. He knows that failure, loss, and suffering, are part of the human condition. They are not to be courted and sought, but in the nature of things they cannot be avoided. He has learned how to grow through his failures: to accept the fact that all his dreams cannot come true. Even suffering he has come to see as an inevitable part of life and growth since man is both mortal and fallible. He is beyond self-pity and free of the habit of blame which makes it necessary for so many people to demand whenever things go awry: "Whose fault was that?" He has learned to see that the failures and sufferings of men can be fruitful in the whole context of things. When at long last two members of an expedition of British climbers stood on the summit of Everest, the leader of the expedition remarked that they had "climbed on the shoulders of all those who went before us and failed." The healthy religious person, seeing his own efforts as part of a larger and longer meaning than his own immediate destiny, can take comfort even in his suffering and failure from the thought that even though his best efforts and greatest strength have not been enough, they have not been wasted and lost. They will have their usefulness through what they add to the sum total of human understanding and experience. The mother does not begrudge the pain it costs her to bring a child into the world. She sees it as part of a much greater process, the creative ongoing force of life itself. It is so with the healthy religious person. Nobody wants to suffer. Everybody must. The man of faith is at least able to believe that his suffering can be creative, that it does have meaning within a larger scheme of things. And from this conviction in time of need he can draw comfort and strength. He knows that he is part of a struggle which is worth making.

The healthy religious person is one whose approach to the world around him and to the people in it is expectant and hopeful rather than critical and negative. Carl Sandburg relates a fable of the old settler in a pioneer town who stands by his gate one evening as a traveler comes along the road. "What kind of folks live around here?" The traveler asks. "Well, stranger," says the settler, "what kind of folks was there in the country you come from?" "Well," says the stranger, "they was mostly a low-down, thieving, gossiping, backbiting lot of people." "Well, I guess, stranger, that's about the kind of folks you'll find around here." Another traveler follows soon afterwards and the same questions are exchanged except that the stranger says in answer to the question about the kind of people who lived where he came from, "Well, they was mostly a decent, hard-working, law-abiding, friendly lot of people." And the old settler replies: "Well, stranger, that's about the kind of folks you'll find around here." The one who expects goodness and courage and strength has a better chance of getting it than the one who expects meanness, cowardice, and weakness. All these qualities exist in varying degree in all of us and we draw out of people something of what we believe to be in them and expect to find. It is an elementary principle, but every parent, every teacher, every doctor and minister, everyone who has to deal with his fellow men, must learn to practice it. Sometimes he will be disappointed, but more often he will be surprised and encouraged by the hidden splendor which does reside within the commonest individual and can be set free by trust and hope. The healthy religious person has learned this lesson.

The healthy religious person has achieved within himself a sound working balance between two seemingly contrary attitudes towards himself: self-criticism and self-confidence. Each of these is essential to health and wholeness. Orthodox Christianity has traditionally put its weight on the side of self-criticism. We must come under "the conviction of sin" before we can be saved. We must acknowledge our sin and through humility and penitence receive forgiveness and absolution. There is truth in this great traditional teaching. A man cannot safely ignore his own limitations, his own mistakes, his own deliberate evasions of what he ought to do. He needs to know that he is human, prone to error and sin, in need of help from a power greater than himself. Only so can he avoid the sin of pride which blinds him to his own humanity and to the humanity of others. Yet at the same time a man must have some proper respect for himself and his own value; some confidence that he is worth something and that he has talents and gifts which can be useful in the world. In the process of twenty years in the ministry it has seemed to me that my task as minister was more often that of helping a person recover his self-confidence and sense of his own worth than of creating in him a sense of guilt for his sins and errors. But however that may be the healthy religious person is one who has succeeded in keeping these two sides of his human nature in sound perspective: his proneness to error and sin on the one hand, his worth as a human being on the other. We all come into the service of the Lord aware of our imperfections, frightened perhaps that we may be unable to meet the demands on us which will be made, but also aware of our strength, confident that we are good for something and ready to offer the best that we have. The healthy religious person knows that he shares in the sin and corruption which are part of the human condition, but he dares affirm his own worth and thus avoids the foolishness of pride while he continues to trust in the usefulness of the powers which he does possess.

The healthy religious person has developed a capacity for the enjoyment of the world and its people. He has an eye for the beautiful, the tender, the delightful, the enjoyable in all the manifold ways in which these qualities express themselves in the world. He is capable of laughter at himself and with others. He has kept a childlike spirit which looks with wonder on the world. His spirit is suggested in some lines from "With Age Wisdom" by Archibald MacLeish:

> At twenty, gazing round about
> I thought the world a miserable place;
> Truth a trick, faith in doubt,
> Little beauty, less grace.
>
> Now at sixty what I see,
> Though the world is worse by far,

Stops my heart in ecstasy.
God, the wonders that there are.*

This is a subtle and contagious quality often lost in the press of modern life. We are too busy to see, too hurried to pause to look at the sea and the sky and the hills and the fields, too lost in ourselves to realize that we live in a world which is crammed with beauty and meaning, a world which is not only to be used and exploited, but also to be enjoyed. The medieval mind was characterized by an attitude which has been described as "the unmercenary love of God." That is to say one could find the real truth and power of religion only if one sought it without ulterior motives, with a certain uncalculating interest and concern. Today we are urged to be religious because it will help us solve our problems, be successful in our jobs, keep us out of trouble, gain the respect of the community. All these are laudable motives, no doubt, yet I think the healthy religious person, while appreciating their value, is religious for none of these reasons primarily. Rather he has found a certain joy and radiance in the midst of life which is so beautiful and true and alluring that he must seek it for its own sake and communicate it to others because he desires that they too may share in it. A medieval tale tells of a woman in France who was seen one day walking down a street in Lyon carrying a lighted torch in one hand and a pail of water in the other. When someone asked her what she was about she replied that with the torch she would burn up heaven and with the water extinguish the fires of hell and then people would love the good God for himself alone and not from desire for the joys of heaven or the fear of the pains of hell. The healthy religious person carries with him something of that pure, simple, and unmercenary quality. Its contagion brings fresh life to a bored and cynical world.

Most of all, the healthy religious person is one who in the course of his life and experience has come to some

* *Songs for Eve,* Houghton Mifflin Co., Boston, 1954, p. 42.

creative understanding and acceptance of Jesus' penetrating statement that "He that will save his life shall lose it and he that shall lose his life shall find it." This apparently paradoxical statement brings the two approaches of religion and psychology very close together. The happy person, the healthy person, the useful person is not one who has simply been relieved of his anxieties, spared the sufferings and tragedies which are part of human life, adjusted himself to the ways of a confused and tormented society. Rather he is the one who has learned how to give himself to something which is worth loving and serving, and in that process of self-giving—the loss of himself, so to speak—has found a new self with greater resources and deeper insights than the old. Life's greatest fulfilments come when we have literally lost ourselves for the sake of something so beautiful and so good that we no longer care what happens to us in the process of serving it. Mental health and religious health consist in being needed and being able in some measure to meet the need. Our generation fears old age not only because of the prospect of illness and weakness and death, but more so because of the prospect that there will come a time when nobody will really need what we have to offer. Not to be needed is the greatest sorrow in life.

Psychological understanding can provide us with the ability to look objectively into our own hearts and minds and to relate ourselves realistically to the world around us. Religion can offer the framework of meaning and the sense of direction which enables us to make creative use of that knowledge.

I do not think it matters a great deal what our theological beliefs are provided they are beliefs which give life great and profound meaning. All formulations of religious beliefs are systems of symbols through which men try to express the magnificent truth that they have found meaning in life which is greater than themselves, and that they feel themselves to be personally part of that meaning involved in it. There is really far more unity among the great religions of mankind and among the various Christian churches than we usually admit. Different as our doctrines and rituals may be, men of good will are close to one another when it comes to the principles by which life should be lived. There is a great direction. It leads from ignorance into knowledge; from conflict into understanding and peace; from indifference into compassion; from hate into love. God has many words to speak, and the variety of human thought and experience is vast. It is not to be thought that God would communicate all his truth to one group of people exclusively and confine the interpretation of his will to one creed or church. More than we need external unity in form and creed, we need that internal unity which enables a man to love his own faith and be loyal to it while realizing that another man may likewise be traveling in the great direction, though he states his faith in different words.

Meanwhile, at the practical level there is need for continuing and increasing cooperation between the clergy and the medical profession. The health of a human being, we are coming to see, is not merely a physical thing. It is made up of the various parts of the whole man: his physical condition, his emotional adjustment, his vocational life, his human relations, his attitudes towards society, and his sense of his own meaning and destiny. Often these things cannot be isolated from one another. We used to think that the body was one thing and the mind or soul another. That, we have learned, is not so. The patterns of health are woven not only out of muscle and bone and blood, but out of thought and faith, friendship and joy, loyalty and sacrifice. Minister and doctor alike—indeed all those who deal with human problems—must learn to see the whole person in all his relationships.

Fortunately this cooperation is increasing today. Out of it is coming a picture of the whole man, the sound and healthy human being that contains at least some of the elements of the healthy religious person I have been describing. He is not an organization man though he cares deeply about his human relations. He is not a machine man though he has made an adequate adjustment to life in a machine age. Above all he is one who has kept his touch with nature and the natural world, with the great traditions of human thought and faith, and with the necessity of giving himself to some worthwhile meaning during the years he is here on earth. He is one whose growth involves the releasing of all his powers in the service of the best.

Twelve On Using All Our Powers

In a most remarkable short story* the British writer C. E. Montague tells of a man in his early fifties who awoke one morning with a curious numb feeling in his right side, which affected him from head to foot. He had lived an active life, achieved a reasonable degree of success, and was alone in the world, his wife being dead and his children grown and married. He saw the numbness as the beginning of age and the dissolution of his powers. He was not a man for suicide but, as he pondered his situation, he came at length to a decision. This moment was an opportunity for him, while his strength and vigor remained, and before he began to decline, to carry out an experiment in which he had long been interested. He was a lover of the mountains and a first-rate climber. He would go to the Alps, where he had often climbed before, and "pursue, right to the end, the piquant experiment of paring and paring away that limiting margin of safety which mountaineers, even the boldest, keep in reserve." He had nothing to lose by such an experiment. No precipice could frighten him any more. He could climb as he had never climbed before. And, when he reached the limits of strength and endurance, that would be that.

So Christopher Bell went to Switzerland to a special place that he had in mind, and one morning some weeks later started out alone to climb a 12,000 foot ridge over the steepest route. He noticed as he started his walk that the numbness was with him in his right leg and arm, but that he did not seem to notice it so much as he went on.

* From *Action and Other Stories*, Doubleday and Company, Inc. Copyright 1929 by C. E. Montague.

By mid-afternoon he was part-way up the ridge, slowly and painfully cutting steps in the ice wall with his axe. He was beginning to tire, and the way ahead was ever steeper and more dangerous. But he felt no fear. Never had the world seemed so beautiful. Never had the zest of climbing been so great. He came at last to a precipitous cliff, sheathed in ice, which was even more steep than the vertical. It had several overhangs which seemed almost impossible to negotiate. But without hesitation he began the ascent, cutting holds for hands and feet with his axe, and holding on against gravity with his free arm. The progress was slow, but at last he reached the most hazardous spot of all: a place where the overhang was directly above him. Progress could be made only inch by painful inch, and at tremendous expenditure of strength and endurance. He began to feel the drag of a huge fatigue, the ache in all his joints, which warned that his strength was failing. And yet, knowing that one relaxed muscle could let him drop hundreds of feet to his death, he went on and on until he reached the moment when he could no longer raise his arm to chop the steps in the ice which were his only safety. He looked up at the overhang still above him, and knew that he could not make those last few feet. And knew also that he had reached at length the moment he had sought.

Suddenly he became aware of something above him, on the upper side of the overhang. He could not see, but he could hear voices, and presently an ice axe came sliding over the edge of the overhang and fell into the abyss below. He knew that somebody was above him, and that whoever was there was in trouble. Then he heard a cry of distress. And new strength began to flow into his arms and legs. He knew no numbness, no cramps, no fatigue. He knew only that he must get up there to give what help he could.

Swiftly and yet carefully he began to climb again, cutting the steps with his axe, pulling himself miraculously upward. And then suddenly he had made it, and saw above him two people: a woman dangling helplessly on a rope, a man above her unable to move from a precarious perch since his whole strength was necessary to hold the woman. Bell came to the rescue and was able to bring these two people to safety. Together the three surmounted the ridge, found a hut, and spent the night in warmth and conversation. Bell had, of course, rescued the man and the woman. But they had also rescued him. For, if he had not heard their distress, he would have yielded to exhaustion and lost his own grasp. Bell told the other man, a doctor, of his recent numbness, and of his experiment.

"Did that numbness cramp you today?" asked the doctor.

"No," said Bell, "but it was there all day except just the time, ten minutes or so, I suppose, when——"

"When you were in action?" said the doctor. "I mean —getting every jack fibre there is in your nature alive and utterly turned on to something outside you, absorbed in it, lost in it, every bit of your consciousness taken up into some ecstasy of endeavour that is passion and peace." The doctor continued: "I guess the great artists, all sorts of them, know how to bring the fit on, or it comes when they are at the top of their form. They seem to get further and further above themselves . . . bring every tissue they have in their being to bear on the effort to get a wee touch to come right. Saints too, I suppose, the real ones, like Francis, the man at Assisi: they have the knack too; they can get more alive; they have found out how to exist at a sort of top pressure. I fancy all of us get just a glimpse of the thing now and then—of what living might be, you know—at a great turn in a game, or when we are in love, or if some beautiful thing in a book bowls us over. Only we can't hold the note, or we can't do it yet: the pitch is too high for our reach; so we flop back into flatness. But we shall get there . . . What we've done since we started as jellyfish is to get more and more of ourselves into action, and we shall go on until we are as much more in action as we are now than when we were jellyfish. Why, in a few thousand years we may be able to live half our time as you lived today for ten minutes."

That is the end of the story, except that Bell decided to stay with life, having found in his ten minutes of total action a justification for anything which might come. And it is true that we are for the most part only half alive. It is true that only rarely do we use all the powers we have and find both the passion and the peace which come with being fully alive and fully in action. It is true too that the real task in life, the religious task, is to find the ways whereby our powers are liberated and we are able to give ourselves, wholeheartedly, joyfully, without reservation to something which is of abiding value.

Fortunately for most of us you do not have to be a mountaineer to know the kind of experience which Montague's story described. It can be known, as the doctor suggests, in other ways. Our powers are released when a certain singleness of purpose takes possession of us. Jesus said: "If thine eye be single, thy whole body is full of light." When we find some value, some cause, some truth which presents itself to us as supreme worth, supreme beauty, supreme necessity, and when we let ourselves go in its service, we do find that we have possibilities of courage and strength and skill which we did not know existed. Much of the frustration and sense of weakness which are so much a part of ordinary life exist because we are of two minds about almost everything. We want to be good but we want to be comfortable too. We want to think and speak boldly but we are afraid of what people will say. We want to see justice done for everyone, but we have our prejudices and bigotries. We want to love and be loved but we are also full of fear, fear lest in loving we become vulnerable and expose ourselves to the possibility of being hurt, fear that our loyalty to what is good will not be rewarded, fear lest we prove incapable of what is demanded of us. Not only are we in conflict because good and evil impulses and desires struggle within us. Our worst conflicts come from the opposition of two ideals both of which are good. Justice is good and mercy is good but often the demands of justice are not the demands of mercy. Truth is good and kindness is good and often the truth is most unkind, and kindness is the lie.

The fact is that we are, each one of us, not single-minded, integrated selves, but many selves, torn by conflicting desires and fears, tormented and weakened by the knowledge that only very rarely have we been able to throw our whole selves single-mindedly into anything, allured by the reflection that when we have been able to do that we have been most effective and also happiest.

There are two possible ways towards this unification of the self, this integration of our various powers, wishes, and impulses. The more familiar one might be called the active, strenuous way. You start out to organize yourself just as you would organize a community group. Selecting among the many desires and impulses which you find within yourself you elect, so to speak, a chairman of the various selves. You give him authority. He is in command and whatever is contrary to him is to be cast out. It is indeed a strenuous way. Jesus expressed it when he said: "If thy hand offend thee, cut it off; if thine eye offend thee, pluck it out." Much of the weight of historical Christianity is on the side of this vigorous, strenuous way of achieving a whole personality. It has been assumed among us that anybody can be good who wants to be and that those who are not are so because they have deliberately chosen otherwise. But anyone who has experimented with this way has found that there are some serious problems here. Our inner selves do not seem to organize as easily as they should and often they reject the chairman who has been set over them. The self thus organized may appear to be unified outwardly while being inwardly in a state of civil war. Too often the strenuous way results in a mechanical integration of the personality which does not represent the loyalty of the whole person. The goodness and the power which emerge from this kind of integration are undeniable. But they are often literal and legalistic, lacking in understanding and sympathy. I have the greatest respect and admiration for the moral power and vigor of the puritan mind, but I should hate to live in a civilization dominated by that mind. For the unification of personality which the real puritan undoubtedly achieves, in spite of its integrity and probity, lacks a quality of flexibility and sensitiveness to the stream of human experience, and also I fear, a capacity for growth and change. Cotton Mather was, no doubt, a very righteous man, strong in his convictions, energetic in his efforts to realize them in his own life and in society, but he belonged to a society which was willing to persecute harmless old women as witches and to participate enthusiastically in the effort to suppress all opinions which did not conform to its own standards. Nobody can do more evil than a really strenuous righteous man who cannot or will not understand.

The other way towards this liberation of our powers, this unification of our lives, might be called the way of self-acceptance and of intuition. The disciplines of this way are different, but no less difficult than those of the strenuous way. The task is not to elect the chairman of the self, throw out the dissenters and organize the rest. Rather it is to explore honestly and deeply this mysterious self and to find out who he really is. The nature of this way is suggested in a letter which was written to Dr. Carl Jung by one of his patients:

> Out of evil, much good has come to me. By keeping quiet, repressing nothing, remaining attentive, and hand in hand with that, by accepting reality, taking things as they are and not as I wanted them to be—by doing all this, rare knowledge has come to me, and rare powers as well, such as I could never have imagined before. I always thought that when we accept things, they overpower us in one way or another. Now this is not true at all, and it is only by accepting them that one can define an attitude towards them. So now I intend playing the game of life, being receptive to whatever comes to me, good and bad, sun and shadow that are forever shifting, also accepting my own nature with its positive and negative sides. Thus

everything becomes more alive to me. What a fool I was. How I tried to force everything to go according to my idea.*

The way of unification through self-acceptance does not require that we do violence to the impulses and needs within our lives which do not fit in with our fixed idea of what we must be. Rather it suggests that we accept these impulses and needs as real and try to find constructive uses for them. There is in all of us, for example, a certain amount of self-love. Of course we are interested in ourselves. What sort of people would we be if we were not? The strenuous way counsels that this is an evil thing, that it must be rooted out and that no matter how we feel inwardly we must present ourselves to the world as in all things perfectly unselfish. The way of self-acceptance suggests that we try to make our self-love useful and creative. We cannot follow the Golden Rule and "do unto others as we would have them do unto us" until we have known ourselves deeply and honestly enough to have formed some idea of what we want done unto us. We cannot truly love others unless we have within our own hearts a real respect for ourselves. The great haters of the world hate themselves first and most.

There is in all of us the ambitious man, the man who is full of the will to power. The answer to this impulse is not to decry ambition and declare all power to be evil. Rather it is to direct ambition towards the best goals and to develop the kind of power which is not tyranny but persuasion based upon love and understanding.

Along with the ambitious, self-assertive person, there is in all of us the submissive, dependent one. Each one of us needs someone or something in the midst of life which can be trusted absolutely, to which we can give ourselves, for which we can spend ourselves, in which we find life's best meaning. Inadequately expressed, this tendency towards submissiveness can lead to the supine acceptance of dictatorship, the spineless conformity of the

* *The Secret of the Golden Flower,* tr. by Cary F. Baynes, with commentary by C. G. Jung, Harcourt, Brace & Co., New York, 1935, p. 126.

slave society, the deification of the nation or the leader or the Holy Cause. But rightly expressed it can be the recognition of excellence and beauty, the knowledge that there do exist realities in the scheme of things before which one should properly be humble and reverent. It is said of Toscanini that on one occasion when he had led the orchestra in a brilliant rehearsal of a Beethoven symphony the whole orchestra rose spontaneously at the end to applaud the conductor. Embarrassed, Toscanini accepted the ovation and then said: "You see, gentlemen, it isn't me. It's Beethoven." This was submissiveness to excellence.

The way of self-acceptance and intuition leads us at length into something very like the Christian experience of prayer. Not the noisy prayer of the strenuous way which besieges God for favors to be granted at once and in full in order that immediate needs may be met, but the kind of prayer, familiar among the great mystics, in which man, having seen himself honestly and accepted himself for what he really is, remains quiet and open to the spirit of God, not demanding anything, but waiting patiently for light and strength to come.

The way of self-acceptance and intuition suggests that often we strive too much and too fiercely for the integration of personality, for the realization of the ideals and goals we have set for ourselves. We begin to use all our powers, perhaps we even begin to experience some of the ecstasy of being fully alive and in action, when we come to see that the issues of life and death are not in our own hands, that we cannot fashion things or persons according to our ideals and plans, but must rather learn to live as creatively as possible with ourselves as we are, with others as they are, and with the world as it is. Paradoxically, our powers are released as we come to care less about what happens to us and more that whatever it shall be we shall accept it without bitterness and acquit ourselves with courage and dignity.

The real lesson of Montague's great story is that the climber Bell, the man who thought he no longer cared about life, found, when he heard the cries for help in his own moments of extreme exhaustion, that he really did care very much, not for himself and his fate, but for life as it was represented in the two people in need. In the moment when he had ceased to care about himself and his own fate, he was gathered in by life and lived more intensely and gloriously than he ever had before. It is probably as well that his story ends where it does. He went back to life, presumably, and what then? Did the paralysis increase, did he decline into weakness and dependency? It might be interesting to know, and he probably did, since all men are mortal. But surely he brought back with him a new reverence and respect for the wonder and mystery of human experience and human capacities. When we have been once thus really alive, the hunger for that kind of life remains and affects all that we think and say and do. We know the reaches of which this life is capable. We know something of the size of the horizons.

The great need for us all is that self-acceptance which can enable us to pull ourselves together, to forgive ourselves and others as we all stand in need of forgiveness, and to begin to live with something of the grandeur and liberty of people who are not ashamed to be what they are. For in that act of acceptance in which we admit with some regret that we are not all that we have pretended to be, there can come also the intuition which suggests that we may be more than we had ever dreamed was possible. It is then that our true powers and possibilities begin to stir within us and we realize that whatever theories there may be for all eternity, the purpose and meaning of this life we now have is plain: it is to be alive, fully alive, as long as we live.

Thirteen ■ The Rediscovery of the Social Gospel

To say that we reject the age of the organization man and the way of life of the "outer-directed" person does not mean that we reject the idea of the individual's social responsibility. One of the weaknesses of the more popular forms of religion today is their tendency either to ignore the vast social and political problems which confront modern man or to dismiss them as soluble through the redemption of individuals. Each person is a part of his society and responsible for its institutions and laws, its administration of justice, its domestic and foreign policies. This responsibility cannot be met by individual goodness alone. The religions of the Western world and Christianity in particular have sought not only the redemption of the individual but the transformation of society. The great prophets of Israel and their spiritual heirs in the history of Western civilization have cried out against cruelty and injustice and oppression as they have been embodied in governments and laws and social institutions. They have insisted that these forces often prevent the individual from being as good as in his heart he longs to be. They have not been afraid to challenge established systems of power in the name of justice and mercy and truth and peace.

The familiar saying that religion must not become involved with politics and economics is a modern prejudice usually found in those who are well-satisfied with the social order as it is. Historically speaking religion has always been involved with politics, unavoidably so, since politics, dealing as it does with human efforts to achieve justice and cooperation in community life, inevitably relates to the moral values which religion teaches. The policies of a government, the laws of a land, do have moral significance. Their effect is more or less justice, more or less peace, more or less respect for human freedom and dignity, more or less brotherhood. Religion cannot afford to be silent and unconcerned about such matters. The Founding Fathers wrote into our Constitution a provision for the separation of church and state as institutions not because they believed that religion had nothing to do with government and law, but because they wanted the church as an institution to be free from government control in order that it might more effectively carry out its role as the conscience of the state, the critic of its policies, the upholder of the moral values to which even the state is answerable. The separation of church and state as institutions implies the relevance of religion to government and law. It is notable that in Communist countries the churches often receive direct aid from the state. This aid is given not because the Communists believe in religious values to which the state is answerable but because they have found that religion is a force in the minds of millions of people and have therefore sought to control the church by controlling the purse strings.

There are today at least four major areas in which the forces of religion must become actively involved in the effort to influence essentially political and legal decisions of governments.

The first of these has to do with the control and eventual constructive use of the tremendous new force of nuclear energy. The new weapons have brought us to a situation unprecedented in all human history. Man's inhumanity to man has been expressed in frightful ways in the past but never before has man had the power literally to destroy his whole civilization, to poison the air that all men must breathe, and even to corrupt and deform the biological structure of generations yet to come. Only the ingrained habit of thinking of war as somehow limited in its destructiveness prevents us from seeing the sheer madness of the situation in which we now find ourselves. Our imagination cannot comprehend the possibility of our own extinction

—not personal, but the total extinction of our society and all that it has achieved. We do not really believe that in the first day of atomic war America would suffer forty million casualties. Yet all the facts are there to corroborate this dread prediction. The civil defense people know it. The scientists know it. The generals know it. The Atomic Energy Commission knows it. Some of them say so. But almost all are reluctant to face the terrible reality, the new truth: we can no longer hope to be victorious in any war. The very concepts of victory and defeat have lost their meaning. We are today required to take steps so new, so foreign to all our previous thinking about the relationships between nations that they seem absurd and impossible. But they are not absurd and they are not impossible when the question for the people of every nation is not victory but survival, not control of the world by this nation or that one, but the preservation of a world fit for the human species to live in.

When Albert Schweitzer made his broadcast appeal to the governments and peoples of the world for the cessation of the testing of nuclear weapons, he was all but ignored by the press and radio systems of America. What the greatest living exemplar of the Christian way of life had to say about the survival of the human race was apparently not news. Yet he called to the attention of those in places of power their terrible responsibility not only to their own nations but to the community of nations. These weapons have brought us to a crisis in the relations among the nations of the world. It is the function of religion as the spokesman for God's love and for man's survival to demand a fresh approach and the creation of effective legal and political controls of the power which can be used either to destroy us all regardless of our political faiths, or to usher in a new day of human progress and welfare. Is it the business of religion to be on the side of those forces in government and in the body politic which are seeking to control the greatest physical force ever released on the earth in the interests of human welfare and peace? Is it the business of religion to promote life or to promote its destruction? Is it the business of religion to be for the poisoning of the air we breathe or against it? Is it the business of religion to arouse the consciences of men to the seriousness and reality of the present crisis or to lull them to rest with assurances that nothing has really changed? Can there be any real doubt as to the proper answers to these questions? And if we answer "Yes, it is the business of religion to put its strength on the side of protecting human life, promoting human welfare, arousing the conscience of mankind to the novelty and gravity of the present crisis," then we must also face the fact that this great task can be carried out only by agreements among governments, deepened understanding of the situation among ordinary people, and the discovery of political means of control. All this is politics, and he who says that religion in this instance must not be involved in politics is really saying that religion must not be concerned for human survival on this planet.

Related to this area of religious concern is another which is equally important and will be with us for many years to come. Barbara Ward in her recent book *The Interplay of East and West* states it in these arresting lines:

> We have reached the quintessence of nationalism, just when, from the point of view of industrial, economic and social organization, exclusive nationalism has become completely impracticable. . . . However, the scale of the folly may help produce new ideas. Our grandchildren may look back upon this age and be grateful to the atomic bomb and the hydrogen bomb because they realize that in no other way could it be demonstrated to a blinded humanity just what folly its arrogant parochialism had become.*

Here the forces of religion have not only a challenge but a special competence to speak out. The leaders of a nation-state, no matter how well intentioned and enlightened they may be, are in the last analysis answerable primarily to the nation-state. Their lowest common denominator is naked nationalism, their highest can be no

* W. W. Norton & Co., New York, 1957, pp. 106-08.

more than enlightened self-interest. For them the state must come first.

But religion is international. It appeals to a universal God and to a moral order which is above all nations, all peoples, all creeds, all systems. Religion speaks, or ought to speak, universally for man, his welfare, his growth, his fulfilment of the divine dignity and nobility which are in him. It is not at all unthinkable that just as we are now accustomed to the notion that a man may have to lay down his life for his country, so in the future a nation may have to reach the moral heights of laying down its life, its nationhood, its sovereignty for the world. No president, prime minister, or secretary of state could ever espouse such a policy as that. But if we are to overcome the barrier which nationalism throws up against the possibility of world peace and world law, some group of articulate and brave people will some day have to be ready to leave nationality as an absolute loyalty behind and affirm that which all men have in common as an overriding interest: the necessity to survive on this shrunken planet.

The forces of religion, concerned as they have been verbally with the idea of one God, one humanity, one world, one human fellowship, are the natural leaders of that movement. If they abdicate that leadership, if they lose themselves in relatively small disputes and differences, whether political, nationalistic, or theological, they will fail mankind at the point of greatest need. The transition from rampant to limited nationalism, from world anarchy to world community, will be a long and difficult one. It will involve innumerable political decisions, many compromises, many policies, which are at best only approximations of justice and peace. The forces of religion cannot hold back for such reasons. They must make it plain that they are committed by their traditional faith, their appraisal of the human situation which exists, their devotion to the values of brotherhood and peace, to the fulfilment of the dream of one world and one humanity. Can religion survive in the world, justify the confidence of men and win their loyalty if it fails intelligently and courageously to meet this problem and point a way through it? I do not think so.

Last year in Los Angeles the District Superintendent of the Methodist Church found that one of the churches in his charge which was in need of a new minister was located in an area where many Negroes were moving in. He decided on a bold course of action. He appointed a Negro to be minister of the church. The white members of the congregation protested vigorously. Forty of them, nearly the whole membership, resigned in a body. But when the new minister came to his first Sunday morning service in his new church he was met by a crowd of nearly five hundred people both white and Negro. The church did not collapse. Rather, a new church was born. The incident is typical of situations confronting churches of all kinds all over the country. "Brotherhood," wrote Norman Corwin some ten years ago, "is not so wild a dream as those who profit by postponing it pretend." The simple truth is that brotherhood is not a dream at all. It is happening quietly in many places, even within the embattled South. Many obstacles remain. Deep traditional prejudices are not quickly and easily overcome, but the fact remains that brotherhood is on the way and no power of segregation and prejudice can ultimately stand against it. The forces of religion to their credit have had much to do with this trend. It is true that there are still many places where eleven o'clock on Sunday morning is "the most segregated hour of the week," but what is notable and hopeful is that many of the people who desire to preserve segregation know and will sometimes admit that they are fighting in a losing cause, bucking the trend of history as it were.

One of the new facts of our world is the coming of life of the colored majority of mankind and the white man's dawning realization that whatever the past may have been the maintenance of the myths of white superiority will be more and more difficult in the future. The task of helping people adjust to the idea of equality, not as an ideal but as a reality, will be a challenge to the forces of religion for many years to come. Inevitably it will involve them in action on the political and economic scene, as it already has in the efforts to carry out the Supreme Court's decision against racial segregation in the public schools. These challenges and opportunities may not be ignored or brushed aside. Religious groups which try to do so will find themselves left behind by history. Again in this area one would hope and expect that the forces of religion will lead the trend rather than follow it.

It is all very well to argue that you cannot legislate equality, that education of the mind and heart must precede brotherhood. This is true as far as it goes. But we cannot wait until the last bigot has been educated out of his prejudices before establishing the conditions which make for equality of opportunity. Often the conditions themselves are educational. Children who have been brought up in integrated schools simply accept the fact. For them it is not a problem but a fact of life. It will be the task of the forces of religion to present brotherhood not alone as the remedy for ancient evils but as an enormous opportunity for the enrichment of our life. Segregation is wrong, not only because it is unjust to Negroes. It is wrong because it is unjust to white people. It deprives them of a whole range of human association from which they could learn much and within which their own thoughts and feelings could be deepened and enriched. The great glory of American society is that our people do come from many races and nationalities with many and varying traditions and ways of life. And the great glory of the world community now struggling to be born is the same. The world is not, fortunately, made up of white Protestant Americans, but of all sorts and conditions of men. The world community cannot afford to be without the special gifts and insights which each race and creed and nation of mankind can bring to the common treasury of civilization. Our missions to Africa and Asia should be not only teaching but learning experiences. Of basic importance is the development of a psychology which is open and teachable. The forces of religion can play an important part here if they will. They can make it plain that whatever the laws and prejudices of men may be, the doors of the church of God stand open to all who come, that each person is valued for his intrinsic worth as a child of God.

I do not see how in the years ahead any Christian body can dare be neutral on the basic issues of brotherhood. Nor do I see how any Christian body can presume to think it is facing the issues by insisting that conversion of persons to Christianity alone and individually can solve the problem. The Christian insight of brotherhood in God has to be embodied in the laws and institutions of society, and the forces of religion are confronted with the necessity of supporting those laws and institutions which best embody it and of opposing those laws and institutions which oppose it. Here again the religious person is going to get mixed up in politics if he carries his faith in brotherhood beyond mere intellectual assent and tries to do what he can to see it realized in actual conditions of the world around him.

Closely connected with the challenge of brotherhood is the crisis of freedom in our day. The forces of religion have said much in the past and present about the dignity of each individual and the freedom which is his by right of his humanity. These are not mere words. There is a real struggle going on in the world between those who are committed to the idea that a man is of no worth in himself and of value only as a part of a vast and complex social machine and those who cherish the faith that a human being contains within himself potentiality for good, seeds of creativeness which it is a crime against society to suppress. Freedom is not only a God-given right. It has a high degree of social utility. The prevailing beliefs and concepts of society are refreshed and revised by a never-ending flow of new ideas—some of them preposterous, some of them dangerous, a few of them truly creative—which arise from the thinking minds of individual men and women. We simply cannot afford to have that process stop. It would mean stagnation and slow decay. Ideas do shape the course of history. When a state reaches a point where it is suppressing new ideas, when people reach a point where they hesitate to express new ideas, the whole state is in grave danger. Progress takes place because large numbers of people are truly free to think for themselves, to express those thoughts to others, to win a hearing for them on their merits, to have them corrected and revised in the light of the criticism of others, and to embody them in the form of experiments and trial runs which prove their worth or their ineffectiveness. If this process stops, growth stops in the whole community. It is for this reason that the forces of religion have an obligation to maintain the free market of ideas. There are not so many truly creative ideas around that we can afford to suppress any of them, even if this means the expression of a large number of not so creative or even downright silly ideas. An act of religious faith is required here. Dare we believe that human beings, if they are free, can draw upon the profound sources of creativity which underly the structure of the world? Dare we believe that most people can be trusted to recognize the good and creative idea when it appears and reject the bad and destructive idea? It is a sublime act of faith, and often practical experience seems to deny it. Yet the case for individual liberty rests upon this conviction.

A century ago the conscience of Western man was challenged by the social problems of an emergent industrial society. The leaders of the Christian Social Movement spoke out against slavery, against the exploitation of the workers, against inequality of opportunity, against the class divisions of society. They spoke and they were heard. The evils which they attacked have not been wholly removed. Poverty and injustice still exist within our economic system. But tremendous gains have been made and it is safe to say that in America today more people than ever before share in the comforts and advantages which our industrial system is able to produce. With the growth of the labor unions and the increasing far-sightedness of management we have succeeded in achieving under capitalism many of the benefits which were promised by socialism. The Christian conscience may not ignore the problems of our industrial society, nor think of them as solved, but it must now turn its attention to the new problems which we have been discussing. In the discovery of the energy within the atom we have let loose a power in the world greater than the power which was let loose in industrialism. We must find the way to control it and use it for man's health and life. In the problem which has been created by the inability of nationalism to organize the peoples of the world for peace, the Christian conscience is challenged to expand its ideas and its sympathies to the point where they include all people on earth. In the rise to power and self-consciousness of the colored majority of mankind, the Christian conscience is challenged to purge the thinking of the white man of old deep-seated racial myths and introduce him into the family of man. In the challenge to individual freedom which has been such a marked characteristic of the first half of the twentieth century, the Christian conscience is called upon to show the way whereby man can be both free as an individual and responsible in his dealings with his fellow men.

These challenges are, if anything, vaster, more universal, more profound than the challenges of the industrial society of a century ago. No religious view which brushes them aside or treats them superficially can hope to prevail. For they are the problems of survival for the whole human race. They are also the sources of much of modern man's anxiety.

Oddly enough it may be that an intelligent, persistent attack on these problems will be an antidote to that anxiety. Vast and complex as the problems are, we shall suffer less if our minds and energies are absorbed in a constructive approach to them than if we simply look at them and deplore their size and complexity. There is real peace of mind in knowing that you are throwing all your strength into the effort to create human brotherhood, or preserve human liberty, or bring world order and sanity a little nearer. Once you have identified a problem and started to do something constructive about it your anxiety is reduced. Your attention is taken up by what you are doing. You have not passed beyond difficulty, but you have left inertia and vague terror behind. You are no longer thinking of yourself alone, and in that very fact there is healing and strength. Among the most satisfying experiences known to man is the feeling of having been of some real use, of having made a significant contribution to the incarnation of a great idea in the conditions of the world as it is. It is part of the healing task of religion that it calls a man out of himself and demands that he give himself to that which is worth serving. I wish I could detect more of this emphasis in the popular religion of our day. It would be a sign that the renewed interest in religious matters is not born of self-centeredness and self-pity but of deep and sincere concern for the Kingdom of God. Living religion calls man to the effort to realize something of the ideal in the world that is.

Fourteen The Uses of Anxiety

The prevalent anxiety of our time is not so much an enemy to be annihilated as a fact of existence to be accepted, understood, and even used as part of the pattern of a meaningful life. Anxiety is fundamental to the human condition. It arises from certain realities which man cannot change. There are no easy formulae for removing anxiety. There is only the possibility that we may be able to live in an anxious world with intelligence, integrity, and courage.

Anxiety can be an awful, crippling burden. But it can also be a certain intense awareness of life and the world. I am sitting in a little glade in the high western mountain country when suddenly a beautiful buck deer comes out of the woods and approaches the stream to drink its clear water. He moves with grace and yet there is a tremendous tension about him. He does not exactly fear me, for I make no hostile motion. Yet he knows I am there and that I could represent a danger. His ears stick up straight. His nostrils scent the air. Every muscle in his body is tense as he walks down to the bank to the stream. Suddenly he stops and looks at me and then, almost as if balancing and deciding between his need to drink and the possible threat from me, he chooses to take the risk and bends his fine head to the water and drinks. Then he raises his head, looks at me again, and with a great bound is gone into the woods again. It is a beautiful sight: this wild creature so perfectly attuned to his environment, so intensely aware of the one discordant element in it, namely myself, so confident of his own speed and strength that he dares drink even in the presence of the possible threat, so fully alive in every inch of his body and in all his senses. I suppose he was anxious, but that anxiety made him fully and magnificently alive.

In the same way the realities of our human condition, anxiety-producing as they are, can help us to live more completely and more sensitively. One of our basic anxieties arises from our knowledge of the fact that life is short, that for each one of us it will have an ending in death. There is nothing we can do about death except postpone it. Nor do we know its meaning or what lies beyond it. We do not even know when death will come. Every day we run risks of death when we go out of our doors, when we cross a street, when we drive a car or ride in a plane or train. The person who would remove these risks cuts himself off from every kind of activity and actually ceases to live. And so we take our chances every day, using what care we can, but always aware that life contains surprises and accidents which no amount of caution can guard against. Indeed, we are so used to living under the possibility of sudden death that we seldom think of it.

Furthermore the shortness of life adds a certain haunting beauty to the world and to our labors and loves in it. We do not have eternity. We have a limited period of time. And so there is a certain urgency in our living. When you see a thing of beauty, look upon it as though you were seeing it for the last time. It may be that you are. When you put your hand to a piece of work, work at it as if there may not ever be another chance like this one to do a creative thing. There is so little time. Death comes too soon for all of us, and yet if we did not have to live with the anxiety of death we might miss much of the beauty and meaning of life. The philosopher Henri Bergson thought that man's knowledge that he must die was a major factor in man's creativeness. Because man knows that he must die he labors the more to put meaning and beauty into his years on this earth. His works of art, his poetry, his buildings, his laws, governments, and institutions are all efforts of man, the perishable one, to leave something imperishable, the work of his brain and his hands. And so there is always a tension between time, as measured in the life of man, and eternity as suggested in those things which last longer than the life of a man, and those intimations and hungers of the human heart and mind which seem to be forever. We shall never escape this tension. And if we were to escape it we would become like the animals, creatures of instinct, well-adjusted to our environment but without any longing to change that environment, to make it better and fairer, and also without that creative inner hunger to grow and become better ourselves. Man must make peace with his mortality in order that he may use the life which is given him well. But the peace which he makes is not a peace of resignation and defeat. It is the peace which comes with his discovery that his life, short as it is, can have significance in a larger pattern of meaning, can become one with the ongoing life of mankind, can enter into the love and purpose of God.

Man not only knows that his life is short. If he has any capacity for self-knowledge at all he knows that his powers are limited. He cannot do all things—not only because there is not enough time but because, even if he had all eternity, there would not be enough strength in him. It is said that Alexander the Great wept because there were no more worlds to conquer. Most of us weep because we cannot conquer the world we know. This can be a paralyzing kind of anxiety in which a man blames himself endlessly for the weaknesses and failures which are part of the human condition. But the facing of your own weaknesses can be a tremendous help, for it enables you to make choices and to use your limited strength where it will do the most good. The major choices of our lives are made possible when we realize that we are limited and must make the best possible use of our limited powers. Once we have outgrown the neurotic anxiety which makes us punish ourselves for being human, the normal anxiety of knowing our own limitations actually helps us to make thoughtful choices.

A third type of anxiety which all men face is what Paul

Tillich calls "the anxiety of meaninglessness." We are filled with an unremitting hunger for meaning. We long to believe that however short our lives, however limited our strength and skill, we are playing a part in a meaningful drama which would be in some measure less significant if we were not there. The rage and frustration of a small child when abruptly corrected by his parents arise from the fact that he usually does not know why, and so the parents' interference with his freedom seems to him outrageous and unjust. The man who is compelled to go on with a task in which he sees no meaning, no value, no usefulness to himself or others, finds that his interest in life is gone and his energies depleted. He may even go mad. The meaninglessness of the rock-breaking task of a Georgia chain gang drove a number of the men to the point where they turned their sledge hammers upon their own legs and broke their own bones rather than continue.

The true picture of hell for modern man is not the ancient one of the great fiery pit in which sinners roast to all eternity. That, with all its limitations, still represents a framework of meaning. Hell for most of us is the task that means nothing and seems to point nowhere; the relationship which neither grows into love nor diminishes into hate but remains remote and sterile; the life which holds neither heights nor depths but is simply an endless boring routine. In the anxiety of meaninglessness the dreadful possibility which crosses all our minds is that Macbeth's description of life (Act V, Scene V) might be true:

> Tomorrow and tomorrow and tomorrow,
> Creeps on this petty pace from day to day,
> To the last syllable of recorded time;
> And all our yesterdays have lighted fools
> The way to dusty death. Out, out, brief candle.
> Life's but a walking shadow; a poor player,
> That struts and frets his hour upon the stage,
> And then is heard no more: it is a tale
> Told by an idiot, full of sound and fury,
> Signifying nothing.

And so we have a passion for meaning. Most of life is the repetition of ordinary day-to-day words and acts: getting up in the morning, washing, eating, going to work, the dishes, the laundry, the grocer, the same people, the same tasks, day in and day out. But we do these things willingly and even with joy because they contribute to a meaningful pattern: the maintenance of an orderly home, the fulfilment of a long and complicated plan of work. Dull and routine as they are we know that they count. If they were not done life would become chaos. The soldier can stand guard duty through a long and uneventful night because he knows that somebody must do this for the sake of the safety of all. The nurse or the friend can sit up and watch with the helpless and unconscious patient because she knows she is part of a plan for the alleviation of suffering. There may be nothing for her to do except to be there, but she knows it is her business, her meaning, to be there if needed.

Life is a process of finding adequate meanings for what we do or propose to do and we find many partial meanings to live by. At various stages of life home and family, the approval of one's friends, the customs of the community or the school, the demands of education and vocation all contribute to the person's sense of meaning. Some men have found meaning in the effort to realize great ideals like those of brotherhood and justice and peace. Others have found meaning in the quest for power or money or social approval and prestige. Whatever meaning proves in action to be dominant in a man's life may be said to be his God, the power within his life to which he is consistently loyal. We make idols in our own hearts of all the persons, goals, and meanings which we care for most. But there lurks in every man's mind the haunting thought that no one of these meanings, nor all of them taken together is quite enough; that there must be a greater meaning which comprehends all lesser meanings, flows through them and gives meaning to life as a whole. This is the anxiety and the hunger which leads us into the search for religious meaning. We should be thankful for this anxiety which impels us to seek beyond all the immediate meanings for the great inclusive meaning of life as a whole, which forbids us to be at ease with partial meanings. Out of this anxiety have come the major religious insights of the human race, its greatest songs, its loveliest poetry, its profoundest love, its noblest heroism.

Each succeeding generation seeks this meaning in the conditions of its own age, in the midst of the problems which beset it. We in this generation must seek it in a context different from that in which our fathers sought it. We must seek it in the midst of the possibility of total war and total destruction. We must seek it in the midst of complex over-organized life in which the individual must fight for his very existence lest he be swallowed up and become a cog in the vast machine. We must seek it in the midst of clashing opinions and beliefs. We must seek it in the midst of political, racial, social, economic, religious struggles. We must seek it as strangers and pilgrims in a universe more vast and mysterious than ever.

However, in the end, we may state our conception of ultimate meaning that conception will be incomplete unless it contains two qualities: an element of grandeur and an element of intimacy. We live always, as Dr. Oppenheimer has said, "on the edge of mystery." We used to suppose in the days of our naive faith in science that the day was not far off when science would unlock all the closed doors, and explain away all the persistent mysteries of the ages. Science has unlocked many closed doors and will unlock many more, but with the opening of each door we enter not a small room but a vast new chamber of possibility with new mysteries to be explored and new challenges to the human mind. Any statement of the ultimate meaning must be open-ended, leading off into reverence, humility, wonder at the size and grandeur of the mystery which surrounds us. Only in such a mood can we hope to understand the smallest part of the meaning of our own lives. Our statement of the ultimate meaning of life must be large enough to include the infinite variety and mystery of the cosmos in which our lives are set. It must be bold enough to declare that it is a cosmos, that somehow it holds together. It must be humble enough to worship while being confident enough to search. I have noticed that this emphasis on grandeur and mystery makes many people uncomfortable. They do not want a world or a life which they cannot fully understand and explain, and so they tend to retreat behind certain beliefs and to refuse to admit that there can be mystery. I am sorry for these people. They will be threatened by each new discovery, each expansion of human knowledge and understanding. More and more they will be compelled to live frightened and anxious behind their little dogmatic meanings. And because they are frightened they will persecute, denounce, condemn, and fight against the future. I am not only sorry for them. I am apprehensive about what they may do to the seekers and pilgrims who threaten their little systems of meaning. Men whose meanings are small will always hate and seek to destroy men whose meanings are great. The bigot is a man of small meanings, afraid of the larger ones which challenge him.

It is not to be denied that there is anxiety attendant upon the acceptance of the world's tragedy and mystery. But it is a creative anxiety. Science is built upon an insatiable but disciplined curiosity. The arts are the efforts of men to express in form and color, in sound, or in words impressions of the life within them or around them which suggest greater meanings than are found in the ordinary day-to-day world. Anxiety is the spur for man's creativity. The anxiety man feels in the presence of grandeur and mystery can change to reverence and humility; it can lead him on into new wonders and possibilities.

This sense of the vast perspective is a part of the answer to the anxiety of meaninglessness. But there is more to the answer: intimacy, the sense of personal involvement which comes as the heart and mind of man are in some way touched by association with the grand perspective.

We may call this sense of personal involvement religious experience. It takes place whenever the individual has the feeling of personal relationship to, responsibility for, or enjoyment of, the whole context of meaning which lies behind his life. This feeling may come to him in many ways: through the enjoyment of nature, through contact with other persons, through the expansion of knowledge, through loyalty to ideas and values which transcend the individual life, through art or science or religion or human service. Religious experience is what happens when grandeur visits the human mind and heart and dwells within their limitations. Christian theology expresses the twin elements of grandeur and intimacy in its central doctrine of the Incarnation. The Word, which is the God who created all things and whose being permeates all things, is, in Jesus, made flesh. That is to say it dwells in human form among men. Every religion which has endured has found some way to express this meeting of the Eternal and the temporal, the unlimited and the limited, the ultimate meaning and the partial meaning as expressed in an individual human life. In Judaism God spoke through the law and the prophets. In Buddhism the holy is constantly returning to earth through the successive re-incarnations of the Buddha. In the mystical sects of Hinduism the disciple withdraws from the demands and pressures of the world in order that he may lose himself and become one with the Ground of all being. Always the process involves some feeling of identity and personal involvement in the grandeur of life's total meaning.

There are many different varieties of religious experience as William James emphasized long ago. People of different backgrounds and temperaments will find religion in different ways. I can do no better than cite here five examples of authentic religious experience and hope that the reader may find in one or more of them something akin to what he himself has experienced but has perhaps not recognized as religious. Each one of these descriptions contains the twin elements of grandeur and intimacy.

The poet Wordsworth found religion and the sense of grandeur and meaning in his apprehension of the natural world. Behind natural beauty he saw meaning with which he could identify himself. In his "Lines Composed a Few Miles above Tintern Abbey," he wrote:

For I have learned
To look on nature, not as in the hour
Of thoughtless youth; but hearing often times
The still sad music of humanity,
Nor harsh nor grating, though of ample power
To chasten and subdue: And I have felt
A presence that disturbs me with the joy
Of elevated thoughts; a sense sublime
Of something far more deeply interfused,
Whose dwelling is the light of setting suns,
And the round ocean and the living air,
And the blue sky, and in the mind of man:
A motion and a spirit, that impels
All thinking things, all objects of all thought,
And rolls through all things.

There are few of us so alien to the beauty of the world, so lost in petty detail, so blind to the order and majesty of nature, that we do not know something of what the poet means. It may have been a fleeting glimpse, a vague intimation soon swallowed up and forgotten in other concerns. But it was there for a moment and it is most important that we realize that all the deepest experiences of life have this fleeting quality. They come and go. But in their comings and goings the mind of man is enlarged, his sympathies deepened, his purposes reinforced, his energies replenished.

Of a quite different sort is the vision described by the Quaker John Woolman, that gentle, implacable Quaker apostle of brotherhood, who a hundred years before the Civil War went up and down the eastern seaboard persuading slave-owners to set their slaves free. He writes in his *Journal* that:

In a time of sickness . . . I was brought so near the gates of death that I forgot my name. Being then desirous to know who I was, I saw a mass of matter of a dull gloomy color between the south and the east, and was informed that this mass was human beings in as great misery as they could be, and live and that I was mixed with them and that henceforth I might not consider myself as a distinct or separate being.*

What we call the social conscience is nothing more than this: the recognition that one is involved with the sufferings and needs of one's fellow men, that there is no escape and no peace of mind except in throwing oneself into the effort to bear some part of the burden of the world's suffering. If you have ever felt pity and sympathy and an imperious need to help the suffering and the oppressed; if you have ever enlisted yourself in the effort to get justice done, to bring about the conditions that make for peace, to realize in practical fact the way of brotherhood, you know something of this kind of religious experience.

A third type of religious experience is suggested in a very famous chapter of the Old Testament, Isaiah 6. Here Isaiah describes how he was called to be a prophet, one who speaks for God in the world. He says that one day in the temple in Jerusalem he "saw the Lord, high and lifted up" surrounded by the Seraphim. So great was the grandeur of his vision that he was filled with shame and fear. "Woe is me," he cried, "for I am undone. For I am a man of unclean lips and I dwell in the midst of a people of unclean lips and mine eyes have seen the King, the Lord of Hosts." Then one of the Seraphim took a live coal from off the altar and flew to the young prophet and touched his mouth with it and said: "Lo, this hath touched thy lips and thine iniquity is taken away and thy sin purged." Then the prophet hears the voice of the Lord saying, "Whom shall I send, and who will go for us?" And he hears his own voice replying, "Here am I; send me." When we get behind the ancient Hebrew imagery we find in this story a most simple and forceful description of the psychological impact of religious experience. When we find ourselves in the presence of something outstandingly beautiful and good, our first reaction is apt to be one of sorrow and shame that we are unworthy of it. God is so

* *The Journal of John Woolman,* Houghton Mifflin Co., Boston, 1871, p. 264.

great, I am so small. But then, small as we are, we are somehow challenged by the majesty of what we have seen and in spite of our unworthiness our fears are removed and when we see what is required of us we are able to answer: "Here am I; send me." We all know what it is to have been in the presence of grandeur, to have been stirred by it, to feel unworthy of it, and at last to be so captivated by it that we give ourselves to serve it as best we can. This, too, is religious experience.

A fourth type of religious experience might be described as intellectual. It is suggested in a very famous letter which the nineteenth-century scientist T. H. Huxley wrote to his friend Charles Kingsley in reply to a letter which Kingsley had written him on the occasion of the death of Huxley's son. Kingsley's letter was full of pious admonitions to the agnostic Huxley to accept the Christian faith. In the course of Huxley's letter in which he thanks Kingsley for his concern but refuses the invitation Huxley wrote:

> Science seems to me to teach in the highest and strongest manner the great truth which is embodied in the Christian conception of entire surrender to the will of God. Sit down before fact as a little child. Be prepared to give up every preconceived notion, follow humbly wherever and to whatever abysses Nature leads or you shall learn nothing. I have only begun to learn content and peace of mind since I have resolved at all risks to do this.

This is the religious experience in intellectual terms: the determination to seek truth and only truth, to follow where it leads, to leave behind all prejudices and opinions and trust only truth itself in the faith that nothing that is true can possibly be contrary to the best meanings of religion. There is religious value in the patient research of the scholar and the scientist. And for each one of us reverence for the truth can be an experience of grandeur and the patient search and experience of intimacy.

There is, finally, a form of religious experience which is not uncommon but is seldom recognized as religious. It is like the religion of Brother Lawrence: simple, intellectually uncritical, intensely practical. Every church, every community, will find a few people among its members who always seem to be there when they are needed. They cheerfully accept the difficult, unpopular tasks. They are not interested in rewards or in praise. I recall one such person, an elderly lady, who had become over the years a kind of mother to all the unfortunate persons who came her way. A new girl in town of foreign extraction and unfamiliar with American ways would find a home with this lady until she could locate a job and get along on her own. The parolee from prison could turn to her for assistance in getting work and starting life anew. She visited the sick, bearing with her on most occasions a tureen of hot soup, or a bowl of fruit, or a book which she thought would be interesting.

Once I asked this lady why she did all these things. Her reply was characteristic of her scorn of theory and her direct concern for human needs: "They have to be done, don't they? And since that is so why shouldn't I do them?" If you had asked this lady whether she had ever had a religious experience, she would have replied, "What's that?" She had never been converted, had never seen a vision, had no "doctrine of God." But it just so happened that at the right moments she was always there, giving concern and service and love where they were most needed. This, too, is religious experience.

All of these types of experience are religious. They are also more common than we usually think. Further, it is well to notice that no one of them is an escape from anxiety but an acceptance and creative use of anxiety. Wordsworth feels the ultimate power and presence not as peace but as "a motion and a spirit, that impels all thinking things, all objects of all thought." It is alive and at work. John Woolman's vision of the dull mass of matter and of his identification with it shatters any feeling of ease and complacency and calls him to action. Isaiah's confrontation by God fills him with shame and then commands him to be prepared to speak harsh words of justice and truth to people who do not want to hear them. Huxley, the scientist, speaks essentially of the scientist's unending hunger for knowledge, his need to search beyond all the safe accepted positions for the new truth which may appear. And the good lady cannot be at peace until she has done what is necessary for those in need.

We are a long way, in these experiences and in the similar ones which touch our own lives from time to time, from the kind of canned religious experience which is so common today. The revival of religion today, if it is a real one, will lead men not out of anxiety, but through their anxiety out into new countries as yet unexplored. Like Abraham who at the call of God went out, not knowing whither he went, so in this strange new world each one must also become a pilgrim again; and, leaving behind his small and comfortable meanings, seek the great and inclusive ones which can bind his world together in brotherhood and peace. For in sharing in these tasks is his only peace.

Fifteen ■ Hope for the Anxious Man

We have recently purchased a television set and one day in my innocence I turned it on just in time to hear a man say to me and presumably to millions of others: "There's nothing wrong in your life that a little more faith in God won't cure. That's what this country needs: a little more faith in God." Who can deny that we would all probably be better off with "a little more faith in God"? And yet, as I heard these words so glibly spoken I could not help thinking of all the individuals I have known who were in deep trouble, and of how fatuous it would have been to explain to them that all they needed was "a little more faith in God." Not that they did not need more faith. They did and we all do. But such clichés are like telling a sick man that all he needs is a little more health, or a starving man that all he needs is a little more food. Such statements are all quite true but hardly helpful in meeting the real problems.

The aspects of the current religious awakening which we have been discussing suggest both the seriousness of man's predicament and the positive opportunities and possibilities which lie before him. In this time of crisis and radical change religion can offer man two possible answers to his anxiety and fear. One is the way proposed by much popular religious teaching today. It is a re-affirmation of the ancient verities in much the same form which they have always had. It is an effort to return to the faith and practice of a simpler age. It calls on us to return to the God of our Fathers, or to the patriotism of our Fathers which makes God and the cause of the nation synonymous. It is sometimes an effort to learn to apply the psychological tricks and techniques, which are useful enough in many trivial matters, to the great issues of life's meaning: "Believe that God will help you and He will." "Believe that it will all turn out all right, and it will." "Believe that you are good and courageous and successful and happy, and you will be." In spite of the vogue which this approach to religion has enjoyed in America in recent years and in spite of the real help which it undoubtedly has given to numerous persons, we cannot forever postpone the question: Is it true? Or is it an escape from the trials and responsibilities of freedom and of thought into the peace of obedience and acceptance of arbitrary beliefs and authorities? An acute observer of American affairs, D. W. Brogan, recently raised the question in these words:

> That there is a genuine religious revival, I do not doubt; that the churches are not in retreat, I do not doubt. I do doubt that the intellectual truce can be kept up indefinitely, in which few people ask, "Is this true?" And there is a practical test coming that will be, I think, decisive. If five years from now, in those areas in which organized religion is strongest, that is, the South—desegregation in the churches is not pretty nearly complete, I shall take the liberty of doubting the existence of a great spiritual upheaval.*

But religion can also offer another way of meeting the terrors and anxieties which beset modern man. It can challenge him to accept the dangerous world as it is, to see the opportunities for growth and change which it contains, to use his freedom and his powers of reason and faith to transform himself and the world, to move ahead in the knowledge that it is human destiny to change, to suffer, to doubt, to question, to experiment and to grow. "That religion will conquer," wrote Alfred North Whitehead, "which can render clear to popular understanding some eternal greatness in the passage of temporal fact." We look in vain to the high priests of popular religion for that sense of "eternal greatness." Their gospel is smoothly presented with all the skills at the command of the public

* "Unnoticed Changes in America," *Harpers Magazine*, February, 1957.

relations men. But it is not a summons to greatness. It is a summons to dependency, conformity and mediocrity. The religion that is needed will be one which calls man to the realization of the potential greatness which is in him, which requires of him that he be as good as in his heart he truly wants to be. It will be a faith which exalts rather than degrades him, encourages rather than condemns him, helps him to solve the problems of the self that he is, not by palliatives, but by the creation of the self that can be and ought to be.

What can such a faith offer the anxious man in his need? This man is each one of us in some measure. We all share his concerns and worries, his doubts and anxieties. This man has been condemned by some as a hopeless sinner; pitied by others as a lost soul; threatened with promises of ultimate disaster; bribed with assurances of eternal bliss. He has been described as a moral failure or as a helpless pawn in a social machine or historical process too complex for him to understand or control. He has come to think too meanly of himself, to doubt his own worth, to question his ability to make any sense of life. I think it is time we gave this man his due. He has his problems, but his achievements and his strengths are not inconsiderable. I want to speak in defense of this anxiety-ridden, fearful, questioning, wondering, spiritually hungry man.

Yes, he is afraid, and rightly so, that with all his efforts he may not be able to avoid the ultimate disaster of a third world war. Yet look what he has already done in his efforts to build peace. He has aided in the construction of a world organization for the purpose of creating the conditions which make for peace. It is a far from perfect organization, but he has stayed with it and supported it and after twelve troubled years it is still alive, more alive than it was at the beginning. Sometimes its deliberations are far beyond him, but he goes in thousands to see them and to watch with surprise and satisfaction the machinery which seeks to keep the peace. This man has no illusions about war. He knows what it is, in most cases, from actual participation. He knows its ugliness and cruelty. He wants peace with all his heart and he is learning, however slowly, that peace can only come out of justice and freedom and a human concern as wide as the whole world. He does not know, and therefore he must live with the anxiety that all efforts for peace may fail, but at least he is beginning to know that the tasks of peace are long, long tasks and that he cannot be at peace in his home in fortunate America unless the things that make for peace are growing all over the world. He is becoming a world citizen. Such growth is slow and painful, but it is going on.

This man lives in terror of the destructiveness of the weapons which he himself has made in order to protect himself. But he knows that there is no real security for him or for anyone in the mere possession of military power. He knows that his most recent discoveries could destroy him and all his works, but he also knows that they contain a promise and a possibility not only for destruction but for the increase of human health and welfare. So he stubbornly continues to believe that he will be able to arrive at agreements with the peoples of other nations for the control and constructive use of the vast new reservoir of power which his science has given him. He is beginning to see that on the achievement of such agreements his very survival depends. And this we may say with confidence of the human animal, as of all other animals: when the question is seen to be that of survival or annihilation, the creature may be counted on to make the choices which he believes will lead to survival. No matter how difficult and precarious life may be, we cling to it tenaciously, hoping against hope that it can be made beautiful and good, believing that it is a precious gift which we may not waste or throw away.

This anxious man may not outwardly pay very much attention to the war of ideas. He is busy with his own small thoughts and concerns. But he plays his part in the war of ideas all the same. He may have his doubts about the strength of the foundations of his own mind but he exhibits again and again a massive good sense of fair-mindedness. How many demagogues have tried to lead him out his apparently incurable prejudice in favor of freedom! How often they have seemed to succeed only to find to their surprise and dismay that this man, who seems so easily led, has suddenly ceased to heed them! It is interesting and wonderful that in America we do not punish, imprison, or hang our demagogues. We let them rant and rave and then turn our backs on them and go ahead with our real business. No force stopped Senator McCarthy in his effort to scare the people out of their freedom. It was just that most people finally grew tired of nonsense and ceased to listen or be frightened any more by what he said. This anxious man is not a hero, but if the experience of the American democracy means anything at all, it means that he can be trusted in the long run to know the difference between the false and the true, between ill-will and good-will, between injustice and fair play, between slavery and freedom. And when he finds out the difference in given instances he can be trusted most of the time to make the positive choices of truth and good-will and fair play and freedom. This man is not a lost soul, but a soul in the process of finding himself.

This man knows that he lives in a world where interdependence at every level is the rule. He has few illusions about being a self-made man. He may regret the decline of rugged individualism in an economic sense, but the benefits of interdependence are too great to be denied and, anyhow, there is no going back. He knows that the interdependence of the modern world means security for him and for all other men. He knows that he must depend upon his neighbors and that they must depend upon him. He guards his individual liberty of thought and speech, his right to have a say in how things are done, but in his heart he knows that he is part of a community of men which embraces the whole world and that he cannot live outside that community. He is beginning to know too that only the spirit of brotherhood and equality for all kinds of men can transform the interdependent social machine into a community of men and women who care for one another. On the credit side for modern man chalk up the fact that everywhere the barriers of race and nationality and class and creed are going down. Here and there some frightened people struggle desperately to keep them up, but their strident voices carry in their very desperation the knowledge of defeat. All men are not yet ready to accept the idea of brotherhood in action, but those who are not know that they are fighting in a losing cause. The interdependent world which the machines have made is here to stay. It must and will be held together by the spirit of brotherhood.

This anxious man wonders often where he himself fits into the whole scheme of things. His life contains many disappointments and much frustration. Often he feels futile and unable to see that life means anything at all. But give him credit for daring to ask the questions, for having the wit to worry about such things. Give him credit for being dissatisfied with little ruts, trivial tasks, mediocre concerns. Give him credit for being a pilgrim and a pioneer, and not an old settler complacent and smug in his isolated clearing. His hunger for a framework of meaning is the fundamental fact in the reawakening of interest in religion today. This hunger is a deep and important need and it cannot be fed with thin broth of clichés and surface reassurances. You can tell this man if you like that somebody up there loves him, that he need not worry, that it will all turn out all right. He may listen for a while with courtesy and even evince some interest. But you cannot feed his real hunger that way. He knows that the meaning of life is not that he is a fawning slave before the throne of some mysterious and invisible oriental potentate. He knows that his "Father in Heaven" is not a sugar daddy. You cannot fool him very long and that fact is to his credit—not his shame. He is not irreverent. His hunger for some sense of the Divine in the midst of his life is very sincere and very strong. What shall responsible and thoughtful religion say to this man in his hunger and his need? I think it should say something like this:

"At the foundations of your life, at the foundations of

all life, at the foundations of nature and of the universe itself there is a blazing, singing unity of meaning. That meaning is creative, it brought the world and all living things into being. Its impulses flowed through all living things as they struggled and failed and developed and grew and survived. Its impulses lifted man out of the purely animal kingdom and started him on his long way. They gave him the capacity to feel wonder, curiosity, a hankering to try new ways and see how they worked. They gave him an everlasting restlessness. They gave him anxiety that he might not be complacent and at peace, that he might not stop growing. They gave him fear that he might learn to survive in a dangerous world. They gave him beauty, joy, art, a sense of adventure, a capacity to be surprised. They gave him faith, hope and love to live by. You and all other human beings are part of this unity and meaning. You are yourself, an individual, yet you are connected with this source of your being as the tiny inlet is part of the vast ocean or as the child is part of the parent. You draw strength from it. Its impulses and urges flow through you. In the world they work through you. You are to them as hands and feet and eyes and ears and brain and heart are to you. This is a framework of meaning grand in its proportions, vast in its depths and as intimate as the love of man and woman."

In such a framework of meaning man can see himself, humbly as he ought to do, with all his smallness and all his limitations, but also with dignity, as a part of a scheme of things which is alive with possibility, rich in variety, permeated with vitality. He is not relieved of all that worries him nor does he avoid suffering, failure, loss, the tragic choices and necessities of life. But they are no longer blind and meaningless disasters. They carry with them "the means of grace and the hope of glory."

Through twenty years of experience in the ministry, involving close contact with the joys and sufferings, the triumphs and failures of all kinds of people, one basic impression remains in my mind: the amazing resilience of human beings, their capacity to meet difficult situations, accept drastic changes in their lives, grow through suffering, and, in Sandburg's phrase, "keep coming." Therefore, though there are sound reasons for the current pessimism about man and his destiny, that pessimism is only part of the story. The other part—and I believe the more important part—is man's incessant restlessness, his habitual questioning of the old ways, his constant curiosity about what lies beyond the horizon.

So I am inclined to feel hopeful about the anxious man of today. To be sure, he faces many and complex problems. Some of them have never been faced by any of the generations of men before him. But if his problems are great—so also are his resources. Technically, he can span the globe in a matter of hours and has made his first experimental efforts to escape the prison of earth's atmosphere and explore outer spaces. The whole world is at his doorstep—no part of it more than a few hours away—and his words and thoughts can be communicated to other men anywhere in a matter of seconds. Thus the opportunities for understanding and peace are as vast as the needs are great. He is plagued by many anxieties and fears—some of them real, some of them created by the very newness and strangeness of the situation in which he finds himself. But his knowledge of himself, of the inner forces which help to make him what he is, and the social forces which help to make societies behave as they do, is greater than ever before. If the growth of the spirit of brotherhood is painfully slow it is well to remember that this is the first century in which it has been possible to put the weight of scientific research and knowledge behind the ideal of brotherhood, and to think of it not as a far-off dream but as biological fact and the necessity of life in this world. If the burden of poverty borne by so many people in the newly emergent nations across the world seems shameful, it is because we are the first generation which has had the resources, the skill, and the courage to believe that poverty can be conquered. If the clash between ideologies—political, economic, religious—seems dangerous and tragic, it is because a genuine confrontation between varying ideologies is now taking place. If modern man wonders whether he can cope with the complexities of modern life, it is because he has so much more to cope with than his forefathers had. His challenges are different, more subtle, but no less difficult than those of the pioneers and adventurers of earlier periods. They demand not only courage, skill, and determination but a far deeper knowledge of the world and of the human mind than has ever been required before.

Modern man is right to take his predicament seriously. He would be out of his head if he did not feel anxious. The challenges which he faces are both difficult and dangerous, but they are not insurmountable and his resources are not inconsiderable. For comfort he can recall that "the great ages have been the unstable ones" and it is in such an age that he lives—an age full of dangers but also full of possibilities.

In Governor William Bradford's *History of the Plymouth Plantation* the author reports that when the time came for the Pilgrims to leave the Dutch city of Leyden where they had lived for many years and to embark on the venture of settling in an unknown wilderness thousands of miles away across the sea, there were many regrets and some profound anxieties. But Governor Bradford describes the response of his people to the situation in two telling phrases: "They knew that they were pilgrims," and "they summoned up answerable courages." A similar necessity confronts us all today.

Nor are we without the spiritual resources here in America to meet the situation. America is dreams and promises, possibilities and new horizons. The religion that can meet modern man's need will be in the great adventurous tradition of the Western world: not the retreat into a new dogmatism or into narrow patriotism or into psycho-religious palliatives or into mass conversion. Whatever else it may be it must be a faith that reminds man that he, too, is a pilgrim and that for all the perplexities and difficulties which confront him there are "answerable courages" in which he can trust. Therefore he need not despair. We are not living in the twilight of man's quest. It is the early dawn. The possibility of an age of terror and destruction is not the only one that lies before us. There is also the possibility of an age of unprecedented growth in human wisdom and human dignity. It is not the end. It is the beginning. And modern man is free to choose the direction in which he will travel. At the very least each one can choose the manner in which his own strength and knowledge shall be used. And in that choice, boldly made and faithfully followed, lie not only the issues of life and death for our civilization but such peace of mind as it is given us in this world to know.

1115